'Are you putting it about that I'm barmy?'

They made us **LAUGH**

A Compendium of Comedians Whose Memories Remain Alive

by **Geoff J Mellor**

Introduced By Arthur Askey & Dickie Henderson

Published by George Kelsall Littleborough

This book is about fifty-two laughter makers – comedians no longer with us.

Why fifty-two? because any one of them could have topped a Variety Bill – one for every week of the year.

Most of them are Northerners – because most of the funny folk come from the North, especially Lancashire and Yorkshire. Blackpool favourites are well represented, because most of these comic 'turns' made a hit there.

Some of these performers literally 'died the death' when appearing south of Birmingham, consequently they got scant attention from southern scribes.

This is an attempt to remedy that position.

The omission of 'Greats' like Harry Lauder, Dan Leno and George Robey may cause a few raised eyebrows, but others have told their story many times.

Most of the material in this book is new . Some of the artistes have never before been documented. But all these performers 'went over big' in their day.

As the author is no 'intellectual', the performers in the book are not subjected to any 'critical analysis'. No attempt is made in the brief biographies to explain why these funny folk did what they did. Being mostly Northerners, it would be safe to assume they simply 'did it for the money' and at the same time escape the rigours of life in the pit, the factory, or the mill. All these occupations are necessary, but they hardly raise a smile, and certainly not on the faces of people who have to earn their living in them....

The entertainers listed in this book have done their 'turn'. During their all too brief sojourn on the Northern Music Hall stage they brought happiness to many.

They are recalled with affection. They are still talked about. Their memory lingers on.

If these pages can be perused without a smile – or perhaps an occasional tear – then 'critical analysis' is certainly indicated...

Geoff J Mellor

© G J Mellor 1982 ISBN 0 9505577 4 9
Published by George Kelsall The Bookshop 22 Church St Littleborough Lancashire OL15 9AA telephone 0706 70244
Designed and illustrated by Ernest Connell Printed by Commercial Centre Oldham

CONTENTS

Foreword by Arthur Askey CBE

Hello Playmates!

Of the 52 artists mentioned in this book, I saw 50 of them work – met 32 of them – and worked with 12. Some of the names will be familiar to readers, but others will fall into the 'never 'eard of 'em' category. So I am more than pleased to feel that this book will recall some marvellous comics – some of whom I had almost forgotten myself. For instance, if you were to have asked the late Jack Hylton, or the late Tommy Handley, or the present day J B Priestley or Arthur Askey who was the funniest comedian they ever saw, the unanimous reply would be – Jimmy Learmouth, whose biography I was delighted to read in these pages. He really was a funny, funny man, yet hardly ever came to London. I only ever saw him in Liverpool, before I entered show-biz myself. As the Author says, in those days, humour was 'zoned' – North and South of Birmingham – then North of the Border.

I remember the first time I met Max Miller when I first went on the Halls, topping the bill as my name on radio filled the Music Halls in their dying days.

Max said: 'I hear you're going to play Glasgow Empire'.

I, very naive in those days, replied: 'Oh yes – why – don't you play Glasgow?'

He said: 'No – I'm a comedian – not a missionary!'

Anyway, this book will prove a good 'read' to everybody, whether associated with the profession or not, as it gives them an insight into some of the great – if not so well-known-performers who 'Made 'em laugh' in what were deservedly called 'The Good Old Days'.

**Dickie Henderson OBE pays tribute
to his late father Dick Henderson**

What a pleasure it is to write about my father, Dick Henderson. He was billed as 'The Comedian who Sings' and, in an era when Music Hall produced total individuals, he was one of the last stand-up comics of his time.

In those days, comics were all completely different from their contemporaries, and yet equally successful. In my father's day, all the material was personalised. No comic used another comic's material. The simple reason was that individual material was only funny when applied to each individual personality.

My father was definitely a 'one-off'. Instead of leaning forward to tell his stories – as English comics are wont to do – he followed the American pattern and leaned backwards. This way, he let the audience come to him...

Dad was very big in American Vaudeville in the 'thirties. In fact I spent my childhood in Hollywood, but Dad said this was no place for a boy of ten and we came back to England. I went to school in South Norwood and my father embarked on a major tour.

Inevitably, when I left school, I went into Show Business. I danced and told stories, my father passing on to me his great experience...

I owe a lot to my father, Dick Henderson.

He was a stout man, with his bowler hat and big cigar, who always closed his act with *Tiptoe Through the Tulips*.

They don't make them like that any more.

To quote Jacques Tati: 'The School Closed'.

Dickie Henderson

*'I want to sing in Opera, I've got that kind of voice. I'd only sing in Opera, if I could have my choice.
Signor Caruso — told me I should do so — that's why, I want to sing in Opera,
Sing in Op-Op-Op-Op Opera! Hurrah!'*

So warbled Wilkie Bard, the man who gave his stage name to the Actor's Card (in rhyming slang) and was positively *the* very first pierrot to earn £100 a week. This fee was paid by Edwin Adeler (of Adeler and Sutton) when Wilkie was invited to tour the pierrot pitches of North Wales, Blackpool and the Isle of Man, as guest artiste.

Considered 'big money' in the early years of the century, this payment was apparently well earned by Mr Bard, for the critics unanimously reported: 'Worth every penny'.

This Lancashire comedian-cum-singer, easily recognised by his stage get-up of curiously high forehead and spotted eyebrows, was born William Augustus Smith in Manchester.

Beginning his working life as a clerk with a textile firm, at the age of twenty-one he began singing and clowning in the 'free and easies' of his native city in his spare time. These venues were places like the Slip Inn, The Falstaff and Liston's Bar, the latter named after the famous Stockport comedian Harry Liston.

In 1893 he finally secured a professional engagement as an 'extra turn' at Ted Garcia's Grand Theatre in Peter Street for £4 the week. Here he appeared as 'Will Gibbard', this being his mother's maiden name.

Two years later, he had reached London, appearing at Collins Music Hall on Islington Green. Here he did a coster study, titled 'My Little Nipper', but this was not really suitable for a Lancashire comedian.

His tour of the London halls was productive, in so much as he appeared on one occasion on the same bill as the great Bransby Williams, a Protean actor of repute. The result was that Will Gibbard became 'Wilkie Bard' and dear old Bransby gave the man from Moss Side a bald wig, at the same time demonstrating the art of Shakespearian make-up to go with his new stage name.

Another meeting was with Frank Leo, a London song-writer, who provided the Bard with *Do You Know any Funny Stories?* and the immortal *I Want to Sing in Opera,* together with a novelty number *Popping In and Out.*

Back in Manchester, local impresario J Pitt Hardacre heard of Wilkie's success, and immediately booked him for pantomime at his Gaiety Theatre. Here, for the 1906 season, Wilkie Bard played Widow Twankey in *Aladdin* with acclaim.

But Bard really found fame when he landed the part of Idle Jack in pantomime at Drury Lane in 1908. From then on he never looked back, his timing, coupled with a fruity voice, improved all the time.

In 1912 he was one of the favoured ones who appeared in the very first Royal Command Performance at London's Palace Theatre. On this occasion he scored a great success with his *I Want to Sing in Opera* speciality.

A tour of America in 1913 brought him £600 a week, but back in this country he could command £250, which was really 'top money'.

About this time Wilkie started specialising in tongue-twisting songs, such as *She Sells Sea Shells, on the Sea Shore* and *The Leith Police Dismisseth Us.*

The Suffragette Movement gave rise to the idea of a song called *Put Me on an Island where the Girls are Few,* which was written for him by Will Letters. Another number Wilkie put over very well was *Chrysanthemums* – about a hen-pecked husband.

The Lancastrian was particularly good at character impersonations – policemen, watchmen, and railway guards were only a few of his specialities, and he continued to make a superb Widow Twankey in pantomime.

Saving his money shrewdly, Wilkie Bard retired early, but was persuaded to make a comeback by Sir Oswald Stoll who put him in his famous *Veterans of Variety* show at the London Coliseum.

And so, Wilkie showed the youngsters a thing or two, and worked happily to the end.

Billy **BENNETT** 1887-1942

'In the street of a thousand bung-holes,
To the East of Limehouse Reach,
Lived a blind Chinese, who loved the sea,
Well, he was the Son of a Peach...'

'He'd a beautiful niece called Wong Wong,
And Wong Wong was yellow all right,
Her father had been, a Royal Marine,
And two Wongs don't make a White...

This was just one of the monologues in the repertoire of Billy Bennett – his most famous being *A Soldier's Farewell to his Horse!* – all delivered rapidly, in a raucous voice. Perhaps the most effective ploy in Billy's comic armoury was his affected surprise at the hilarious effect his pearls of wisdom had upon his audience.

'Almost a Gentleman' was Mr Bennett's billing, and his appearance (on the stage, that is) certainly lived up to it. Wearing crumpled evening suit, a dicky-front that popped out, a red spotted handkerchief round his neck, a lady's garter for a fob, together with hob-nailed boots, he certainly presented a comic appearance.

He topped the lot with a walrus moustache and wore his hair in a quiff, the whole effect when he came on stage was such that the audience was in stitches at his appearance, before he got down to saying anything.

It seems the hob-nailed boots were a legacy of his army days, and which he carried on into his music hall act. In fact, Billy's first appearance on the Halls after his demob from the First War was in the guise of a soldier in dress uniform, but he soon discarded that for the off-beat evening suit, although he kept the army boots.

Billy Bennett, it appears, did just about everything by halves. Born in Liverpool, he was the son of one half of a comedy team called Bennett and Martell, who, Billy was proud of telling, had appeared in pantomime at Drury Lane.

Billy began his stage career as a half himself; not half an act, but the hind legs of a pantomime horse. He ended his career by becoming the Mose half of an act called Alexander and Mose.

The identity of these black-faced comics was supposed to be a secret, and so it was when the act was first formed in 1930, for sound radio at Savoy Hill. At this time Alexander was played by a straight actor named James Carew, but when the act migrated to the music halls two years later, dear old Albert Whelan, the Australian, donned the mantle of Alexander to become Bennett's partner.

Unlike many performers, the Liverpool comedian was not averse to giving advice to up-and-coming comics. His 'Three Point Plan for Success' in the realms of being a burlesque comedian or monologuist could be outlined as follows: 'Never laugh at your own gags – always maintain a sphinx-like countenance.

'Never stress or over-emphasize a point – let the gag do its own work.

'When the laugh comes, don't wait for it to die down before starting again – catch the tail end of it, and try and make your act one continuous ripple of laughter.

Billy's final plea was for sincerity on the part of the comedian. This factor, he said, 'came over' in the act, and was 'the watch-word of success'.

Also unlike many comedians, Billy never had any 'problems'. He was never morose, melancholy or 'difficult' off-stage. In fact, someone who knew him very well during his last years spent in Blackpool said that Billy Bennett was always the 'Gay Bachelor' in real life, and lived it up until the end.

It seems he put down his unmarried state – perhaps that too could be said to be half of something? – to his sojurn in the army. Billy got on well with the ladies in spite of never standing before the altar. In fact, he once described himself as 'God's Gift to Lonely Women!'

Mr Bennett certainly distinguished himself in the Army. In the First War he served with the 16th Lancers and was awarded the DCM and the Croix de Guerre. Typically, this was something he never referred to, either in ordinary conversation, or in his monologues.

'Almost a Gentleman' was surely an understatement.

Reg BOLTON 1884-1955

'Meet me Gwen, on Shipley Glen, On Sunday afternoon,
By 'Number Nine' we'll have a good time, It's just the place for a 'spoon'...'

A tall, lanky comedian is reciting from the stage of the old wooden Shipley Pavilion. The time is the summer of 1906 and the droll with the drawling delivery is anxious to impress in his first season for Sam Wilson at this popular West Yorkshire venue.

Born at Eccles, the lanky Lancastrian had made his initial debut in concert party at Harry Leslie's Rusholme Pavillion, near Manchester, in 1904, and he was engaged at Shipley on a 'trial turn' basis.

Topical material was Reg's speciality, and *Gwen of Shipley Glen* was no exception. But for strangers to the locality, some explanation is necessary in regard to this ditty. Shipley Glen is a well-known beauty spot, and 'Number Nine' is a huge rock sited there – a popular rendezvous for courting couples.

Reg Bolton himself certainly found romance in Shipley, not however near 'Number Nine', but at the rival venue nearby, the Alfresco Pavilion at Frizinghall, where he was engaged for the 1907 season. Here he fell for the charms of pianiste Dorothy Belmore, whom he later married. She was the sister of Susie Belmore, then a soubrette, but later on a notable principal boy (and girl) in pantomime.

At the time of the Frizinghall engagement, the girls had graduated from Harry Tempest's School of Dancing in Birmingham. Later, they teamed up with vocaliste Vera Vere and formed a trio billed as 'We Three' to tour the Halls. This act broke up when Dorothy married Reg and Susie made a name for herself in pantomime.

Reg Bolton also did well in pantomime. His very first appearance was as Buttons in *Cinderella* for the great impressario Francis Laidler, at the Bradford Prince's Theatre in 1909. Principal boy in this production was Florrie Forde, who gave Reg much encouragement, and later on was to play a big part in shaping his future career. Reg Bolton subsequently appeared in fifteen pantomimes for Francis Laidler, most of them in his own favourite role as Buttons.

After the First War, when Gilbert Payne (who had hitherto written many pantomime scripts for Florrie Forde) decided to produce and appear in his own shows, Florrie Forde had no hesitation in co-opting Reg Bolton to fill the breach, which he did very well.

Florrie Forde always went down very well in pantomime at the Dewsbury Empire, where she made many return appearances. At one point she recruited an unknown local girl (from Ravensthorpe) to play principal girl opposite herself. She was Aleta Turner and Florrie, delighted with her success, gave Aleta a three-year contract! (Aleta later married Chesney Allen, at the time partner in a double act called Stanford and Allen, but later with Bud Flanagan as part of the Crazy Gang at London's Victoria Palace.)

Besides writing scripts for Florrie Forde, Reg Bolton toured the Halls as a comedian, appeared in Summer Shows for Ernest Binns at Morecambe, and did very well in revue for Francis Laidler. Billed as 'The Laugh Salesman', one particular success was the revue *Glad Eyes* which toured for years in the pre-Talkie era of the 1920's. In pantomime Laidler teamed the lanky Reg with an equally lanky lady – Marion Dawson – the latter specialising in Widow Twankey parts.

In later life Reg returned to writing pantomime scripts, and also to produce pantomimes, all with great success. He did seven in all for R S Stephenson who was in control at the Dewsbury Empire, the last being *Babes in the Wood* during 1954/55.

In his touring days, Bolton was known to stage hands at the various theatres as 'The Dewdrop Comic' the reason being that he felt the cold intensely! Usually he worked in an unscripted sniffle or two during the course of his act.

The Eccles-born comedian relied on situation comedy and gestures for laughs, in the main, but privately he was fond of telling what he said was a true story of an occurence during his early days in seaside concert party.

One afternoon at this particular resort, the rain came down heavily, and Reg and the other male pierrots stayed in their dressing tent playing cards. At five o'clock they were leaving the tent to have tea when a bedraggled little girl appeared from nowhere, pressed a penny into his hand, and said earnestly: 'Mr Bolton. It has now stopped raining. Will you do your funny sketch, please!'

Charlie **CAIROLI** 1910-1980

Charlie Cairoli – or Uncle Charlie – was resident Clown at Blackpool's Tower Circus so long that people began to regard him as part of the Tower!

For thirty-nine seasons he reigned supreme in the seaside ring – idolised by the children who came back to see him year after year – but when breathing difficulties caused him to cut down his act in 1979, he had to take things easy.

They would be content if he would just walk on and off for the 1980 season 'so they could bill him as appearing' but it was not to be. The resort's best-loved clown took his final curtain before the season commenced.

Charlie certainly came from a long line of Cairoli's. His accent was part French, part Italian, and part Lancashire. But he did not need language. His antics spoke for themselves. The art of the Clown is universal.

Back in the 1870's one of the Cairoli family was Prime Minister of Italy.

Ten years later, a troupe of them were billed as 'Les Cairolis, Premiere Jungleres et Equilibristes' in the French circuses.

Charlie himself made his debut in the circus ring at the tender age of ten, dressed as a page boy, with a black face.

Both his parents were white-faced Musical Clowns. Charlie's job at this time was to suck a lemon in front of his father, who played his clarinet regardless, while mother tootled away on the saxophone.

Musical clowning was always Charlie Cairoli's speciality. At five he could play the saxophone and the xylophone. Later on he claimed to be the only clown to reach high C on the trumpet.

He came to Blackpool via a pantomime in Birmingham. With his father Jean Louis, and his brother Philip, they made up 'The Cairoli Family' who appeared in the 1938/39 pantomime *Cinderella* at Birmingham's Theatre Royal. In the cast were Tommy Trinder and Elsie and Doris Waters.

They were 'spotted' during the run of this pantomime by Blackpool producer Clement Butson and booked for the 1939 season at the Tower Circus.

Blackpool suited the Cairoli's so much that at the end of the season they bought a boarding house in the resort. Charlie, who had married Violet Fratellini (of a rival circus family), kept the boarding house. His children were born there. Regina in 1940, Mary in 1943 and Charlie Junior in 1946.

The Cairoli's did well to establish themselves as favourites in Blackpool, for they followed the ever popular Doodles (William McAllister), who made fun with huge bladders and was a leading light in the resort's Carnival.

In 1947 the father, Jean Louis Cairoli, decided to return to France. Brother Philip went to Canada, so Charlie teamed up with Paul Freedman, the first of several 'Paul's' before Charlie Junior joined the act in 1970. Jimmy Buchanan joined the Tower Circus in 1953 and later became one of the Cairoli 'stooges'.

For his long success in the Tower Circus ring at Blackpool, Charlie owed a lot to his stooges – Charlie Junior and Jimmy Buchanan. Jimmy, of the dead-pan face, has been at the receiving end of more custard pies and jets of water than most folk have had hot dinners!

The children loved Charlie. In Blackpool they followed him about. He would not wear the Clown's traditional make-up for fear of frightening the little ones. Instead he stuck to a red nose, a Chaplin-style moustache and bowler hat, and the whole heap of talent that went to make up his stock-in-trade.

Children were Charlie's life. Just how much his little admirers loved him is illustrated by this true story.

One day Charlie found a little dog tied to the stage door of the Circus. In its collar was a letter that read: 'Dear Charlie. Mam says I can't keep Snowball in the new flats, so please find him a nice house to live in.'

Charlie was very moved by the note and took action. He soon found the young white labrador a good home in the resort.

Mr Cairoli may have been *A Right Charlie* (as he appeared in a TV programme) but he was kindness itself. He was well described by a reporter as 'The Clown Prince with the Heart of Gold'.

Jimmy CLITHEROE 1916-1973

'Pull into the side, Sonny'

Many a young policeman has stopped what would appear to be a schoolboy driving a black Bentley car between Blackpool and Manchester, only to find that it contained the ageless Jimmy Clitheroe.

This 4ft 2in character drove for nearly seventeen years between his bungalow home in Bispham and the Hulme Playhouse studios for recordings of his famous *Call Boy* and *Clitheroe Kid* series on sound radio thus attired.

Jimmy always maintained that the Eton collar, schoolboy cap and blazer, shorts and socks get-up enabled him to play the part of the eleven-year-old 'terror' so much better. His clothes were his 'props' and the studio audience expected him to dress the part. And how they loved him!

During that period, between 1955 and 1972, the shrill-voiced comedian recorded 300 shows and wore out three 'stage mothers'. His first was Renee Houston, the second Patricia Burke, and the third Mollie Sugden who also did the TV series with him. For a long time he had an admirable foil in Danny Ross, from Oldham, who played Alfie Hall, the hapless boyfriend of the Clitheroe Kid's big sister.

At the peak of his popularity, the *Clitheroe Kid* series on sound radio had an audience rating of 14 millions, but when this figure dropped to around 1 million the BBC decided to rest the show.

This decision upset the pint-size Lancashire comic, who protested: 'There isn't a cleaner show anywhere. I cannot understand it'.

But the BBC were adamant and Jimmy had to play the clubs and do 'one-night stands' until he collapsed from fatigue in a hotel bedroom. His tiny frame would not stand the pace, but he kept his exact age a secret till the end.

Born James Robinson Clitheroe; as a schoolboy in real life at Blacko near Nelson in Lancashire, he appeared in Winston Metcalfe's concerts in the village. Then he won a talent competition staged by George Baker at the old Alhambra in Nelson, dancing and playing the accordion.

This gave the Clitheroe Kid a taste of show business and, after appearing again in cabaret at the Imperial Ballroom, local newspaper magnate Harold Coulton of *The Nelson Times* launched him on a professional career by getting him a part with the touring Winstanley Babes.

When this tour finished, Jimmy took a job in a Nelson bakery, until Vi Terry came to the town in touring revue and got him an audition with John D Roberton, the impresario. The latter liked the boy accordionist and got him a part in the revue *Highlights of Blackpool* which starred comedian Roy Barbour.

In 1937 he appeared in a show with Tessie O'Shea at the Central Pier in Blackpool, playing an accordion bigger than himself. As a 'second spot' he played the saxophone and did a tap dance – the comedy was yet to come.

But the sense of humour was there, for when Nelson folk on holiday in the resort recognised him and asked him why he left the bakery, Jimmy would reply: 'Because I didn't make enough dough!'

1940 saw the boy from Blacko in films – playing junior stooge to Arthur Lucan in *Old Mother Riley and her Daughter Kitty* – made at Blakeley's Manchester studios.

With the film part, Jimmy Clitheroe seemed all set for stardom, but this turned out to be a damp squib. For the next fifteen years he did the long, hard slog of the Variety theatres, playing a Little Boy act, similar to Wee George Wood.

The 4ft 2in wonder was very popular in pantomime. He made a very good Tom Thumb! But it was his *Call Boy* series on sound radio that sent him to the top, followed by *The Clitheroe Kid* which ran to 300 recordings. It was a sad day for the shrill-voiced little comic when the show was taken off. He never got over it.

Many children were disappointed when the 'cheeky schoolboy' comedian had to withdraw from pantomime at the Davenport Theatre in Stockport for the 1972 season. And how Jimmy hated letting them down, but the little comic was ill.

Known as 'Skip' to his intimate friends, Jimmy remained a bachelor. He was devoted to his widowed mother, Mrs Emma Clitheroe – their real name, not a stage name. Jimmy died only a few days after the death of his mother.

Although Britain's shortest comedian became the star of the longest-running situation comedy series on radio, Jimmy kept his Nelson twang until the end.

Only he could say: 'Some mothers do 'ave 'em!'

*'Ladies and Gentlemen. Introducing, for your edification and entertainment,
the peripatetic virtuoso of ambivalent vocalisation –* The Great Coram
– in other words a Ventriloquist!'

So might Chairman Leonard Sachs have introduced a notable act, that is if Mr Sachs (of TV's *Good Old Days* fame, at the Leeds City Varieties) had been functioning in the 1920's – when Coram was Top of the Pops in the ventriloquil line.

Coram, whose name was really Tommy Whittaker, was born at Boulder Clough Farm, not far from Elland in West Yorkshire. He began his working life in the textile trade at the West Vale Mills – reputedly at the age of seven – but soon developed a flair for music. He became a boy cornettist in a local brass band and also sang soprano in chapel choirs.

It was obvious that the Yorkshire textile trade could not for long hold down such a lively character. At the age of fourteen he ran away from home to begin a career as a ventriloquist atop a step-ladder on Morecambe sands. His interest in this type of entertainment had been stimulated when a kindly uncle gave him a doll puppet for his birthday. Every night little Tommy practised talking with the figure beneath the bedclothes until he fell asleep.

When the season finished at Morecambe, he became a 'general utility hand' in a travelling circus, and this took him to Northern Ireland. He became a pierrot at Portrush for £3 a week under the name of 'Le Roi', continuing his ventriloquist speciality with a Chinese figure.

Back in England, in the 1900's he toured the northern music halls as a 'vent', and in 1905 came under the notice of Tom Barrasford who then lived in Leeds.

Barrasford ran the Leeds Tivoli, and also a syndicate of music halls, including the Lyceum Theatre in London. After an audition in Leeds, Barrasford offered the Yorkshire vent a week's engagement at the London Lyceum – on a 'trial turn' basis. However, the young man from Elland stayed a month – his salary increasing every week!

In connection with the Lyceum booking, his son Billy Whittaker (now a famous comedian partnered by his wife Mimi Law) tells a good story of how his father got his stage name.

Apparently Barrasford suggested that the up-and-coming ventriloquist should have an agent and made some arrangements. Tommy duly presented himself at a certain London office. The agent there did not fancy either 'Tommy Whittaker' or 'Le Roi' as being suitable for the stage personality he had in mind.

Both were stumped for an alternative until the agent glanced out of the window and saw a street sign which read 'Coram Street, W1'. The agent said immediately; 'From now on you are Coram'.

And Coram he became, and very soon The Great Coram . . . .

While other vents had coster or nautical dummies, Coram set a fashion in having (before a back-drop of Buckingham Palace) a military figure called Jerry, who appropriately sang:
'My name is Jerry Fisher, one of the Old Militia,
'One of the rank and file, no wonder ladies smile,
'For I'm every inch a soldier...'

Jerry was not just another stage figure, but a work of skilled mechanical precision. Tommy Whittaker's love of engineering was reflected in the fact that Jerry worked by remote control – mouth, head and arm movements – all independently of his master. The climax of the act was when Jerry walked off the stage at the conclusion of the conversation. What a finish!

Coram himself was very interested in pioneer flying, racing cars and motor cycles. He loved to race up and down Blackpool sands with Jerry in the jockey seat of a racing car he designed himself, and was delighted to share his interest with a relative by marriage. The latter was also a ventriloquist – name of Gillin.

In later life, Coram took things easy as a gentleman farmer near Clacton, but the mechanical wonder called Jerry found a permanent resting place in the Science Museum at South Kensington.

Not just a 'Gottle of Geer' act – Coram and Jerry...

Billy DANVERS 1889-1964

'The last of the red-nosed comedians of the old
school' and 'A front-cloth comic with a vast
repertoire of gags about booze, dirty weekends
and the mother-in-law', was a well-known
Lancashire entertainer.

That just about summed up Billy Danvers who
died in a Manchester hotel whilst engaged in Don
Ross's famous *Thanks for the Memory* show at the
Victoria Theatre in Salford.

Born in Liverpool, of a well-known theatrical
family, William Mikardo Danvers made a brief
appearance at the age of four on the stage of the
old Tyne Theatre in Westgate Road,
Newcastle-upon-Tyne, with his father Jimmy.
However, his real stage debut as a comedian was
made as a 'trial turn' at the former St James'
Theatre in Manchester in 1908 – about a mile
from where he died 56 years later.

Then in 1910 the Manchester-based Bass
Brothers, Frank and George, roped him in as a
deputy when George got an offer to appear solo in
touring revue for Harry Day. And so young
Danvers became Billy Bass, joining Frank in the
double act, and gaining valuable stage experience.

In 1912 Billy went solo himself, still as Billy Bass, when he joined George Hall's Merry Japs for a summer season at Morecambe.

Billy met his wife during that first season at Morecambe. He was fond of telling the story of how the happy pair were married at noon at Lancaster Registry Office, had just time for a quick sausage and mash dinner, then a rush back to Morecambe where the young bridegroom was due to appear at the two o'clock matinee in the wooden Arcadia on the Figure Eight Park!

After the First War, our man reverted to his original name of Danvers, and as Billy Danvers appeared in Fred Karno's comedy companies. In 1924 he was in the Karno revue *The Love Match* playing opposite lovely Jean Allistone, later married to Tommy Handley.

In his bill matter Mr Danvers was described as 'Always Merry and Bright' and he certainly lived up to that reputation. He was as full of humour off-stage as he was on, and kept his associates happy.

Billy did five very successful summer seasons in the Isle of Man, and as many again in Blackpool, where he was a particular favourite.

In all, he appeared in five Royal Variety Shows, and sang a song *Kiss Me* which he wrote himself. This stood him in good stead for many years and was an accepted part of his repertoire. Although his material seldom varied, he was a universal favourite on the Halls.

During 1961 Daniel Farson, son of American writer Negley Farson, and author of the book *Marie Lloyd and Music Hall* hired the old Metropolitan Theatre in London's Edgware Road (complete with Ivan Dozin and pit orchestra) and made a record of several old-time artistes performing 'live' on its stage.

Posterity owes a great deal to Mr Farson for this enterprise, the result being a record entitled *The Music Hall LP* (Phillips International). This captured for ever the sound of performers like Danvers, G H Elliott, Hetty King, Albert Whelan, Ida Barr, Marie Lloyd Jnr and Hughie Diamond.

Inevitably, Billy Danvers sang *Kiss Me* on this record, and did a sample of his patter, which went something like this: 'Three men... Three men stood in a pub having a drink, you know, all boasting about their wives – and it's not often you'll find a man boasting about his wife – especially if she's not there...'

'One said: 'My wife has the most beautiful eyes in the world; they're pale blue'. Another man said: 'That's nothing. My wife's got lovely eyes as well, they're grey eyes'.

'So they turned to the third one and said: 'Tom, what's the colour of your wife's eyes?. He said: 'I don't know. I've never noticed. I should have done. I've been married long enough' and it worried him.

'So he went home, but he couldn't find her in the slavery – sorry the kitchen – so he went into the lounge and there she was, sitting on the settee in her dressing-gown, reading. So he went up to her, looked her right in the face, and said: 'Brown'.

'And at that a feller got up from behind the settee and said: 'How did you know I was here?'

Bunny DOYLE 1896-1955

'One of the finest pantomime comedians ever to tread the boards'.

That was the considered opinion of the great Yorkshire impresario Francis Laidler, and he was referring to Bunny Doyle, to whom he gave his first real break into show business. Bunny never looked back after his start with Laidler and his droll style and homely wit made him a firm favourite with young and old alike. He certainly deserved his billing of 'Minister of Idiotic Affairs'.

Bunny more or less 'adopted' the Yorkshire village of Giggleswick – where, he always said, they were fond of playing tiddley-winks with man-hole covers – and he had a string of gags about the place which he used for West Yorkshire venues.

A great favourite in his native city of Hull, Bunny was always sure of a warm welcome at either the Tivoli or the Palace Theatres – and he was a frequent visitor to both. When performing in this territory he varied his material accordingly. Giggleswick was dropped in favour of Brough – pronounced with a 'huff' not a 'how' – as Humberside folk well know!

Born in the Third Port, and the son of a Portland Place barber, Bernard (Bunny) Doyle won a prize in a talent competition run by H E Tadman's Uniques concert party at their open-air pitch on the sea front at Withernsea.

Bunny was on holiday as a treat for his twelfth birthday, and this novel experience gave him an appetite for show business. Even when he left school at fourteen and became a GPO telegraph boy, his heart was with the pierrots.

Young Doyle was keen on sport also, and succeeded in getting 'signed on' as a professional footballer by Grimsby Town. He tried hard, but was disappointed when he was only considered good enough for the reserve team.

Then he persuaded George Morgan who ran the Bijou Music Hall in Hull's Kingston Square to put him on one Friday night as a 'trial turn'. He went down very well with his songs and patter, and the next thing was that Mr Morgan had introduced him to the leader of the Sunrays concert party, who were short of a comedian.

Bunny Doyle passed his audition and away the budding comedian went on a tour of the northern music halls. There he gained valuable experience.

Came the First War and the Humberside comedian enlisted with a battalion of the West Yorkshire Regiment and was soon in action in France. However, his comic abilities were quickly recognised, with the result that he became the 'star turn' with the Regimental concert party, known as The Duds.

Bunny was the 'star turn' on the field of battle also, for he was awarded the Croix de Guerre for 'Conspicuous Gallantry'.

In the Second War, more than twenty years later, Doyle toured with ENSA as a comedian, and appeared in more than fifty shows abroad for the troops. In the Middle East he was aboard a train which was blown up, but he escaped unhurt.

During 1941 he appeared in a film made by Butcher's Film Service entitled *Facing the Music.* In this typically British concoction he appeared opposite Betty Driver, the Rochdale-born comedienne, nowadays a firm favourite in the long-running *Coronation Street,* in which she plays Betty Turpin.

After the War years, Bunny Doyle returned to work in his beloved northern music halls as a comedian, but in 1954 he tried his hand at character acting, taking part in the touring play *The Love Match.*

In 1955 impresario Jack Hylton wanted an understudy for Arthur Askey, appearing for the season at the Blackpool Grand Theatre, and Bunny Doyle got the part. However, during rehearsals, Bunny became unwell, and sadly the Humberside comedian did not recover from his illness.

Although comedy plays were a good medium for Bunny Doyle, it was pantomime which appealed to him most. He was very well liked in the business, and a typical gesture ocurred when he was playing at Bournemouth's New Royal Theatre in pantomime.

There word reached him that 108-year-old Mrs Eliza Whitehead was too frail to be taken to see the show. Immediately Bunny chartered a taxi and put Charmian Innes (playing principal boy) and several other leading lights in it. Then, with himself and several chorus girls in his own car, they drove to the old lady's bedside – and put on a 'special version' of the pantomime just for her!

Norman EVANS 1901-1962

'Good Morning, Mrs Brown, Nice day.
Ooh..Oh. Dear Me!
Sorry about that. I slipped — fell off me brick...
Aye. That's better. Both on top now.
Far more comfortable...
It's that tom-cat you know. I'll kill it if I get hold of it.
Whew. It does whiff...I could smell it in t'custard on
Sunday!'

'What did you say? That woman at number seven?
Is she...? Gerraway!
Well, I'm not surprised. Not really. She's asked for it...
I knew what she was as soon as I saw her!
And that coalman. I wouldn't put it past him, either...
Not since he shouted 'Whoa' to his horse from her
bedroom window!'

Fanny Fairbottom, mop-capped harridan leaning
over a back-street wall, is gossiping. She is having
trouble with her ample bosom, which at one stage
becomes wedged between two bricks! The
audience at the Wakefield Opera House is in near
hysterics. This was the usual audience reaction
wherever the act appeared.

Described as 'The greatest Pantomime Dame.
since Dan Leno' Norman Evans was in great
demand for his Dame speciality in pantomime
and his solo act in Variety.

He did a superb 'second spot' comprising a
hilarious sketch 'At the Dentist's' in which (with
the aid of a screen) he played the dual role of
dentist and patient.

To the dentist's assurances that 'This isn't going to hurt' came howls of anguish from the hidden victim, the act closing to roars of laughter when the dentist finally emerged in triumph, holding a giant molar between 'prop' forceps!

Norman's encore was often an amusing scene with a glove puppet, a lovable little Panda named Teddy, with which he held an animated conversation.

The son of a Rochdale organist, Norman Evans was for many years a Methodist lay preacher. He began his working life as a five shillings-a-week office boy at the Arrow Mills in Castleton, later becoming a salesman and insurance agent.

In his spare time he was a prominent member of the Rochdale Amateur Dramatic Society, putting on shows, and also appeared at 'smokers' in the area. Norman also gained experience with a local concert party called The Corruptimists, the name being a corruption of The Co-optimists of West End fame in the 1920's.

The idea for 'Over the Garden Wall' came from a backyard clothes line, but it was a screen in the dressing-room at the Prince's Hall in Sowerby Bridge that inspired 'At the Dentist's' which was first tried out in a Dot Greaves show put on there.

Gracie Fields first saw Norman Evans doing his Amateur specialities when she topped the bill in a charity show at the Rochdale Hippodrome in 1931. This was to raise funds for the Rochdale Football Club. Norman was a supporting act on the bill and Gracie was most enthusiastic. She suggested he could turn professional.

This came about in 1934 after Gracie had cut twenty minutes out of her own act at the Chiswick Empire to give Norman 'a taste of Variety'. Sir Oswald Stoll got to know, the result being that the budding comedian was given an audition at the London Alhambra. This he passed with flying colours and was given a contract. At this, the Rochdale paper tube salesman's salary jumped from £7 a week to £70!

Norman Evans and his stage sketches fairly took the Variety world by storm and only three years after turning 'pro' he was 'first turn' at the Royal Variety Performance of 1937. He appeared in further such shows in 1947 and 1951.

In 1949 he took his homely brand of Lancashire humour to America. He went down well and did a 'spot' in *The Ed Sullivan Show* in New York.

Back home he toured with great success in the revue *Good Evans* and introduced his daughter Norma to audiences at the Leicester Palace as a vocalist.

But the Rochdale comedian's real love was pantomime. He starred in the longest-running pantomime ever, at the Leeds Theatre Royal. This was when he was partnered by Betty Jumel in *Humpty-Dumpty* in 1944/45 which ran for twenty-two weeks – from Christmas to Whitsuntide – and set up a record which is unlikely to be broken.

He had Francis Laidler to thank for this, and it was the Yorkshire impressario who first gave him a 'break' in pantomime. At Keighley Hippodrome in 1937 manager Bernard Beard telephoned Laidler to tell him that he had never heard such laughter in a Variety theatre. Mr Laidler was impressed and invited Norman to appear as Dame in pantomime for him. This turned out to be *Aladdin* at the Prince's Theatre in Bristol.

Apparently the empty theatre was very cold during that December of 1937, and at dress rehearsal Francis Laidler sent out for hot soup and bread rolls for the company.

Norman Evans was sitting there in his Dame outfit and unthinkingly made as if to wipe a drop from the end of his nose with his apron.

Mrs Annie Evans, sitting with her husband to help him learn his part, immediately called out: 'Norman, don't you dare. That's a 'prop' not a hanky!'

Sid FIELD 1904-1950

In March, 1943 Captain George Black – of the famous Sunderland family – launched a new revue at the Prince of Wales' Theatre in London.

Its title was *Strike a New Note* and it eventually ran to over six hundred performances, bringing fame to several 'unknowns' who took part in the show.

Among them were Derek Roy, Jill Manners, a very young Morecambe and Wise (as chorus boys) and an obscure comedian (then pushing forty) who in the next few years rocketted to the top.

His name was Sid Field, and George Black, as producer, had no hesitation in starring him again in a follow-up revue at the same theatre in 1944.

This was *Strike it Again* which gave a great start to the careers of Billy Dainty and Wendy Toye. This in turn was followed by *Piccadilly Hayride* in which Terry Thomas gained fame as second comic to Field.

Then, when well established as a comedian, Sid Field entered the arena of films, starring in a lavish, Hollywood-style musical made in Britain titled *London Town* with Pat Kirkwood supplying the glamour and much attention focussed on a child star named Petula Clark.

In 1949 Field made another picture *Cardboard Cavalier* in which he played opposite Margaret Lockwood. This later effort was 'panned' by the critics, one of them describing the picture as 'an abysmal failure'.

Any failure connected with the film was not due to any lack of talent on Field's part, but simply that the movie-moguls had provided him with the wrong type of vehicle. Perhaps the fact was that films were not the right medium for this particular artiste, who was schooled in the Music Hall tradition.

Born Sidney Arthur Field at Sparkbrook in Birmingham, Sid as a youngster dressed up as Charlie Chaplin to amuse his fellow schoolboys.

At fourteen he left home to join the touring Kino Juveniles and, after some stage experience, became a stooge to comedian Jack Herbert, with whom he toured for some years.

Then he joined George Norton and partnered him in a golfing sketch on the Halls. This was in touring revue around 1930.

When this tour ended Sid went solo as a comedian, and 1933 found him billed at the Finsbury Park Empire as 'The Destroyer of Gloom'.

The next decade saw him doing the hard slog of the music halls without much recognition, but his luck changed in 1942 when he was joined by Jerry Desmonde as a partner in the act. Then the old golfing routine was revived with great success.

The new partner – real name J R Sadler from Redcar – had started out in show business with his brother under the style of Jack and Jerry Desmonde. The latter made a superb 'straight man' and in later years worked with Norman Wisdom.

With Sid Field the golfing routine took on new life with Jerry feeding him such lines as 'Prepare the tee' (reply: 'I hate the stuff') and 'Address the ball' (inevitably: 'Dear ball...') The sketch was now titled 'Following Through'.

Later they thought up a snooker routine, which was equally successful, in fact with the addition of Alfie Dean as 'the Marker' it was included in the Royal Variety Performance of 1946 and was particularly well received.

It was while appearing in pantomime in Nottingham with Jerry Desmonde that George Black saw Sid Field and gave him the vital part in *Strike a New Note*.

In *Strike it Again* the Sparkbrook comedian introduced his famous 'Slasher Green' speciality. This was based upon a wartime 'spiv' character, with extra-long overcoat, trilby worn at a rakish angle, and shoulders padded so heavily that Slasher nearly toppled over. 'Stand well back, Son' was the catch-phrase.

Slasher Green was truly the Pride of the Elephant and Castle and, after Field's early death, Arthur English followed on with a similar character dubbed 'The Prince of the Wide Boys' with equal success.

After the *Cardboard Cavalier* fiasco on film, he returned to the Prince of Wales' Theatre, scene of his previous triumphs, to appear in a stage show called *Harvey* which involved a giant rabbit of that name. Sadly, he was soon absent from the production, due to illness.

Sid Field's well-known song *You Can't Keep a Good Dreamer Down,* together with all his famous sketches, went into *London Town*. Whatever shortcomings the picture had in intrinsic value, the film remains as a permanent record of his talent and a tribute to his memory.

George **FORMBY Snr** 1878-1921

'Coughing better tonight'

This was the pathetic gag of Old George Formby, used when one of his frequent bouts of coughing assailed him on stage. He fought a losing battle against chest trouble and first told the gag at the old Ardwick Empire, during some banter with Dick Hardwick, the popular musical director there at the time. Some years later Dick was shocked to hear that Old George had coughed for the last time.

The Lancashire comedian had collapsed whilst appearing in John Tiller's comedy pantomime *Jack and Jill* at the Newcastle Empire. He was carried to the green room, but efforts to revive him were in vain. A great comedian was at rest.

George Formby was one of the greatest names in show business – and there were two of them, father and son – but it was a made-up name.

James Henry Booth was born at Ashton-under-Lyne, and at the tender age of twelve was apprenticed as a blacksmith's striker to a Manchester firm of ironfounders. The work was far too heavy for his puny frame and the sulphur fumes played havoc with his chest.

As a teenager he was very miserable, to all accounts, and only lived for his spare time, when he sang comic songs and strummed on an old banjo.

On holiday at Blackpool he had a go at entertaining with Cyrus Bell's Minstrel Troupe on the sands. There he palled up with comedian Barney Parsons, becoming his 'feed'. The pair got on so well that they decided to try their luck on the music halls and toured for a time as 'The Brothers Glenroy'.

The act broke up when Barnaby decided to become a traveller in fancy goods, while James went back to singing in the 'free and easies' in the Manchester area. (In later years Barnaby married and with his wife and family went back to entertaining. They became very well known in Morecambe as 'Papa Parsons and the Seven Lucky Lancashire Lassies' the latter being his daughters. His two sons became performers also. One of them, Charlie Parsons ran troupes in Blackpool.)

During 1897 Danny Clarke, proprietor of the Argyle Theatre in Birkenhead, heard Jimmy Booth singing away in the Hen and Chickens singing-room in Manchester. Clarke liked Booth and signed him up to appear for a week at his hall for £2. Danny Clarke did not think 'J H Booth' a suitable name for a music hall comedian, so after seeing 'Formby' chalked on a line of coal trucks, this was substituted. As George Robey had shown an interest in The Brothers Glenroy, so 'George' was adopted also. The result – George Formby billed at Birkenhead!

Not long after this, the great Walford Bodie signed up George to provide a little comedy relief for his Royal Magnets, then at the Lyceum Theatre in Blackburn, with a tour to follow.

Playing the Wigan Empire, George met and married Eliza Hoy, and his luck changed.

He made his home with his wife's family in Marsh Lane, and succeeded in getting a regular weekly engagement at the old Peoples' Palace in St Helens. And so, with thirty shillings a week and his tram fare from Wigan, Formby began married life. Then, through the kindness of Leoni the Cat King, George was signed up to play the Stoll Tour of nine halls at £8 a week. The Wigan comedian was on his way...

Described as 'The Simple Lad from Wigan' Old George Formby appeared with a pallid face, enormous boots, check scarf and suit with pocket flaps turned inside out. He made gags about Wigan Pier and sang *Standing at the Corner of the Street*.

However, due to Eliza's influence, his act became more refined down the years. A new song *John Willie, Come on!* went over well, especially when playing London halls.

When appearing at the Argyle again in 1904, the joyful news came through that Eliza had presented him with a son, also to be called George Formby. At this, Danny Clarke made Old George promise that if Young George went on the stage he would perform at the Argyle Theatre on the occasion of his 21st Birthday.

Young George did keep this 'advance date' at Birkenhead in 1925, but then sadly Old George was not around to see the event.

In 1979 the author called to see Mrs Eliza Booth, following her 100th birthday, and asked the Grand Old Lady to tell a typical gag used by Old George Formby.

Mrs Booth thought for a moment, and then said: 'My late husband was born at Ashton-under-Lyne and always got a great reception when he appeared at the nearby Ardwick Empire, which he did many times. There was always friendly banter between himself and Dick Hardwick, the musical director, who had been there many years'.

'My George would come on stage, point to Dick, and say: 'Look, he's still here – getting ten pounds a week for wagging a little wooden stick. Why, for half that money I'd wave a telegraph pole!'

George **FORMBY Jnr** 1904-1961

With his little ukelele in his hand – or was it a stick of Blackpool rock? – George Formby Junior, was inimitable, irresistable and irrepressible!

He was brilliantly described by one critic as follows: 'With a carp-like face, a mouth outrageously full of teeth, a walk that seems normally to be that of a flustered hen, and a smile of perpetual wonder at the joyous incomprehensibility of the universe and the people in it, Mr Formby has that foolish simplicity which one likes to think is a better protection from harm than all the wisdom of the worldly.'

The oldest of Old George's many children, George Junior was apprenticed to be a jockey at the age of ten, but increasing weight eventually put paid to that plan.

However, during his spell at Ayr stables in Scotland, as a teenager, came his first meeting with his wife-to-be Beryl Ingham, then partner in a girl dancing duo on the Halls billed as 'Beryl and May'. The meeting took place at a picnic arranged by the Popplewell family, on Ayr Green, quite near their Pavilion Theatre.

It was talking with Beryl at this time that convinced George about launching himself as a solo act upon the music halls. This he eventually did at the age of sixteen, at Kemp's old Earlestown Hippodrome, as a supporting act in a programme which contained silent pictures and Variety.

This initial appearance was under the name of 'George Hoy' (his mother's maiden name) on the advice of a family friend and performer – Harry Lauder. (It was not until some time after his father's death that George would allow himself to be billed as 'George Formby'.)

Single-act George did not cut much ice on the northern music halls of the period. In fact, according to his friend and stage partner Sam Paul, George 'got the bird' in Blyth whilst appearing there in a revue titled *Chip Off the Old Block*. Young George was most upset at this, and mother had to be sent for from Wigan before he would go on again.

After that episode Sam Paul taught him some comedy material, and arranged for George to buy a ukelele from a hard-up pro when the show reached Barnsley Empire. (Sam Paul was an ex-Catlin Pierrot, and an expert of the banjo and ukelele.)

In 1925 George Formby met up with Beryl again, this time at the Castleford Queens' in a show put on by Tom Convery, entitled *Formby Seeing Life.* In this revue George had Jenny Howard as his leading lady and the girls from Darwen, Beryl and May, were dancers in support.

At Castleford George 'popped the question' and Beryl became his wife and stage partner, when need be. They became inseparable and, like Formby Senior, Young George's luck changed with marriage. He played the London Alhambra for Sir Oswald Stoll and there added a catch-phrase to his act which stuck down the years – 'Turned Out Nice Again?'

Then came the famous songs written for him by Gifford and Cliffe – *Cleaning Windows* and *Mr Wu* – followed by Noel Gay's immortal *Leaning on a Lamp Post* and other numbers written by Alf Cotterill of Doncaster.

In 1934 George appeared in his first talking picture *Boots, Boots* made by Blakeley's of Manchester. In this film George sang *Why Don't Women like Me?* and Beryl danced to *Chinese Laundry Blues.*

Then came a series of twenty pictures which rocketted George Formby to fame. These included *Keep Fit, Trouble Brewing* and *Keep Your Seats Please.* In 1938 he is said to have had a film contract worth £100,000. Young George appeared in three Royal Variety Shows, the last being in 1941.

But, like his father, Young George fought a losing battle against ill-health.

With the son it was heart trouble and, following a collapse in 1951, he was under doctor's orders to take things more easily.

In 1960 the sudden death of Beryl upset and un-nerved him.

A few short months later the famous ukeleles were silent, and a confused little Lakeland terrier named Willie Waterbucket sat among the effects at the big house in St Annes (called Beryldene) which was up for sale.

The curtains had fallen for the last time on Young George Formby...

Tom **FOY** 1861-1917

'Ay, I am a Fool. We've coom, Me an' 'Im'.

A performer dressed as a country bumpkin, with open-necked jersey, and wearing a conical dunce-like cap, makes his way on stage leading a donkey.

The year is 1911 and a packed house at the Doncaster Palace roars a welcome to the man and his moke, who are making a quick return visit to the newly-opened theatre in Silver Street.

Tom Foy is the man in question – billed as 'The Yorkshire Lad' – and his animal companion is 'Baley' which is short for 'Balaam'.

The title of his act is 'The First of April' which accounts for the opening line 'Ay, I am a Fool' and the rest is soon made clear.

Tom introduces his four-legged friend by saying: 'This is Baley – my little Baa-Lamb! Ah rescued thee from the bondage of a circus, didn't I lad? An' tha's been wi' me ever since, ain't that right, Baley?'

'Ay, no circus tricks for thee now, Baley lad. Tha's too old'.

'But tha' cooms in at stage door jus' tha same, doesn't tha? No coomin' in at scene dock for thee!'

'Tha's still a performer for all that. Ain't that right, Baley?'

Tom Foy's material is very simple, but he draws upon his circus background to clown about. The donkey was equally simple, but sagacious. Apparently it brayed and sat down to order, and shook its head when spoken to. Needless to say, the pair were great favourites in pantomime.

A critic who saw Tom Foy's act reported: 'His ridiculous mannerisms and absurd sayings keep the audience in an uproar all the time he is on stage'.

Although billed as 'The Yorkshire Lad' it seems Tom Foy was born in Manchester, of Irish parentage. He was the eldest of four brothers, and served his time as a sign-writer.

Then the family moved to Halifax in Yorkshire, where Tom set up in business painting and lettering wagons and farm carts, in the Shroggs Park area of the town. Very often he was called upon to letter circus vehicles, and this whetted his interest in performing.

Joining a travelling circus as a scenic artist, he learned the 'business' of a clown, which training he found of great use later in his career. It was while the circus was touring Ireland he met up with Ernestine Matthews, a girl tumbler, who later became his wife.

Very soon a new act was formed, billed as 'Ernestine and The Three Foys', Tom being joined by his brothers John and Joe. Then Eddie joined in, together with nephew Alf. When this happened, Ernestine persuaded Tom to go solo with the donkey. She then continued with the act, re-formed as 'The Five Foys'.

That enterprising entrepreneur, Mr J Pitt Hardacre of Manchester, was then alerted. After seeing Tom perform, Hardacre immediately signed him up to play Idle Jack in *Dick Whittington* at his Gaiety Theatre in that city during 1900.

In that pantomime Tom formed a friendship with the great black-face artiste Eugene Stratton, who persuaded Foy to try his luck in London, getting him an engagement at the Oxford Music Hall. This went down well and a tour of the Syndicate Halls was arranged. Tom Foy and his Donkey were on their way.

They had appeared in seven pantomimes – one in London – and Tom had been approached about Drury Lane, but then came bouts of illness. Tom Foy was fifty-six when he collapsed at the Argyle Theatre in Birkenhead during 1917.

At the time he was touring with a company in a sketch called 'Hunting Trouble' and his wife Ernestine and his brother John carried this on to fulfil the remaining engagements, one of which was at the Halifax Palace.

During his stage career Tom Foy made twenty gramophone records on the old Zonophone label. He certainly put Sowerby Bridge (a suburb of Halifax) on the map with his *Farewell to Sarby Brig* in which he refers to living at Chapel Cottages.

And Baley? He ended his donkey days in a stable in Manchester's Oldham Street – near the famous Hen and Chickens singing room – within sight and sound of music hall performers to the end...

Lounging against the piano, singing about *The Old School Tie,* and between songs exchanging with the pianist his very own brand of 'carelessly witty humour', the 'Aristocrat of Entertainers' Ronald Frankau cut a distinguished figure in his immaculate tail suit, which seemed to go well with his bald head and suave manner.

The son of Arthur Frankau the composer, young Ronnie spent his early life in the Cambridge district, later moving to London. His mother was 'Frank Danby' the Edwardian novelist, while his brother was the well-known Gilbert Frankau.

Ronald shocked his family when in 1911 he joined the chorus line at Daly's Theatre as a singer, after passing an audition. On tour *The Maid of the Mountains* took in Liverpool and there the Eton-educated Frankau found himself next to Tommy Handley. The pair struck up a friendship which was to last a lifetime.

When the tour finished, the young Frankau went to Canada with just £20 in his pocket, to seek fame and fortune as a journalist. However, when war broke out in 1914 Ronnie was soon back in Britain to enlist. He became a captain in the Royal Artillery and served both in France and India.

During his service career he saw many concert parties sent out to entertain the troops and this revived his interest in show business.

Upon 'demob' our man was anxious to set up as a concert party entrepreneur, and for a start took over two pitches in the North East in 1919.

One was at beautiful Jesmond Dene (near Newcastle-upon-Tyne) and the other at Whitley Bay. At Jesmond he transformed what was simply a canvas tilt over a wooden platform in a rustic setting into The Playhouse. There he put on many shows and in its new guise the old 'Dinky' was to last through many chequered years until in 1970 the University Theatre at Barras Bridge replaced it.

The Whitley Bay venture concerned The Kursaal in Marine Avenue. Will Ambro and George Houghton had been running this, but in 1921 Frankau acquired it and changed the name to The Playhouse also.

Concert party companies formed to perform at these venues by Frankau included The Purples, The Blues and The Rag Dolls, before he hit the jackpot with his famous Cabaret Kittens in 1923. Then Ronnie disposed of his theatres.

After a season at Whitley Bay, the Cabaret Kittens went on tour and John Wilshire booked them for their first engagement at the Royal Hall in Harrogate, where they were a great success. In fact this company went from strength to strength and for the 1925 season they were at The Sparrow's Nest in Lowestoft, in direct opposition to Wallis Arthur and his company, who were at the Olympian Gardens.

It was at Lowestoft that Naunton Wayne joined the company of 'Kittens' and very soon made a name for himself as an entertainer and impressionist.

Frankau performed himself of course, and Wayne did a very good impression of him. So much so, in fact that when later in the season Naunton transferred to a company in Paignton, an unsuspecting critic rang up Ronnie to tell him that 'A chap down in Paignton is pirating your act!'

Other famous personalities associated with the Cabaret Kittens included Nan Kenway (later partnered by Douglas Young) and Cecil Fredericks, who left to join Harry Korris and later became 'Ramsbottom' in the famous *Happidrome* shows.

The 'Kittens' produced some notable pianists. Conrad Leonard went on to become Musical Director at the Lyceum Theatre in London; Leo Conrish wrote songs, and Monte Crick (Frankau's accompanist) who became 'Dan Archer' on the radio in *The Archers*.

Ronald Frankau was anxious to break into broadcasting, and when his Cabaret Kittens were booked for a ten-minute outside broadcast from the Chatham Empire in 1927 he was delighted. But he was not so delighted when he received the fee, which was the princely sum of one guinea for the whole company!

However, the episode had a brighter side, as it led to a renewal of his association with Tommy Handley. In 1930 the two were paired together in *North and South* in which the down-to-earth Liverpudlian and the Old Etonian exchanged topical patter over the air waves. In 1934 this act became 'Mr Murgatroyd and Mr Winterbottom', and they became masters of quick-fire patter, both on the radio and stage.

Everyone was shocked by the sudden death of Tommy Handley in 1949 – the nation's favourite radio star in *ITMA* – but none more so than his old friend Ronald Frankau, who completed his remaining engagements in Variety and retired to Eastbourne.

There he put a brave face on things by telling Pressmen: 'The public don't seem to appreciate my style any more.'

Frank E **FRANKS** 1894-1974

Frank E Franks could have been the Billy Butlin of the North.

It's a fact that in 1930 this cherubic little man got the idea of building a holiday camp of chalets at beautiful Crimdon Dene, on the North East coast, but the Depression was on and no one would back him in the project.

Billy Butlin, however, utilised the idea at Skegness five years later – with results we all know – and got a knighthood thrown in.

Back to Frank E Franks: The second in a family of twelve, the bare-foot boy from Hebburn-on-Tyne eventually appeared before royalty, in two Royal Variety Shows.

As Francis Kane he began work, straight from school, in the pit at Houghton-le-Spring. Afterwards he said that getting the sack from that job was the finest thing that ever happened to him.

This came about when the pit was on strike and the 16-year-old pit boy took a temporary job singing at Bert Velma's Imperial Cinema at Bill Quay, between the reel changes. (This type of act was known as 'a lantern cooler').

When the pit strike was over, Frankie decided to continue his part-time singing stint by performing at the various little Picture and Variety halls in the North East, to supplement his meagre miner's pay packet.

All went well until a pit deputy sat in the audience and recognised him.

Then it was the sack for Frankie. As the deputy said: 'No man can do two jobs'.

This proved a blessing in disguise, for that fine old Shields showman Richard Thornton heard about the incident and sent for him. After an audition, Mr Thornton booked Frank E Franks (as he called him) for his North East chain of Empires, as a singing comedian.

During the First War the lad from Hebburn served for a time in the Durham Light Infantry. Upon arrival at his base, the CO took one look at the new five-feet, one-inch soldier and told 'Little Frankie' to report to the Entertainments Unit.

In the 1920's Frank E Franks reported to 'the guv'nor' otherwise Tom Convery who in those days had an agency in the Westgate Road area of Newcastle-on-Tyne.

Thus Little Frankie resumed his career in touring revue. He also developed a flair for script-writing, which Convery recognised. The result was a revue titled *Demobbed* which proved a first-class vehicle for the talents of fellow Tynesider Albert Burdon, who appeared in this revue for a long time, playing the lead opposite Vi Vivienne.

A later revue he wrote called *Love Birds* starred Little Frankie himself, and in it he appeared opposite a willowy blonde from Langley Moor named Ruth Kitson. Convery changed her name

to Gene Boyne and she became quite well-known as a male impersonator and principal boy in pantomime.

In her act the former Miss Kitson was Eugene, the Dandy, and in real life she lived at a place called The Boyne – hence Convery's inspiration for her stage name. However, Little Frankie changed her name again when he married her!

The revue *Love Birds* toured successfully for three years, and this fact inspired Mr Franks to put his own shows on the road. After this, he wrote *Take Cover,* took it out himself and made money, and with the proceeds took over a dog track in Easington.

When well established as a comedian in the 1930's Frank E Franks became an impresario, producing and running his own shows at the old Victoria Hall in Toward Road at Sunderland. At this place the top admission price was six old pence.

Sad to relate, a Nazi bomb finished Sunderland's 'Old Vic'. When this took place, Mr Franks transferred his interests to Stockton-on-Tees, where he produced fourteen pantomimes in as many years at the Globe Theatre.

In his long career, Frank E Franks claimed to have appeared at every music hall venue in the North, and in 1952 he decided to bring the curtain down for the last time when his touring revue *Gentlemen, The Queen* concluded its run at the West Hartlepool Empire.

At that time Mr Franks had completed fifty years on the stage. After that, he only made very occasional club appearances, 'to keep his hand in'.

In 1972 he told the author he was working on his memoirs.

I was privileged to see the manuscript and found the contents fascinating.

However, I could not fail to notice one glaring omission.

This was that every year he had invited 2,000 poor children from Teesside to see a special pantomime matinee he put on at the Globe Theatre in Stockton...

Freddie **FRINTON** 1911-1968

How many comedians graduated from the Pierrots to the Palladium?

Not many I reckon, but Freddie Frinton did it – although it took him all of thirty years to do so. In addition, he became a star on the television, in the series *Meet the Wife* playing opposite Thora Hird.

Two years before he died, the author interviewed him in his dressing-room at the Bradford Alhambra, where he was playing Baron Hardup in pantomime. There he pointed to a picture of Jimmy Slater's Super Follies at Cleethorpes and told me: 'Yes that's me on the left, with Jimmy Slater himself on the extreme right in one of his glamourous female impersonations. The year was 1935 and the pay £3 a week. Not bad for a concert party comic in those days'.

The son of a Grimsby fisherman, Freddie Hargate began his theatrical career singing in the clubs of his native town. Then he tried comedy and got an engagement at the old Theatre Royal in Sheffield. Then came the Super Follies at Cleethorpes for a few seasons, until War broke out.

After service in the Forces, Freddie toured the Halls with George Black's famous show *Stars in Battledress,* before he struck out as Freddie Frinton, solo comedian.

His chief stock-in-trade was an hilariously funny sketch entitled 'Dinner for One, Please, James'. In this concoction he played the part of a manservant to an autocratic old lady, who forever changed her mind at the dinner table. In the sketch, Freddie used to manage to trip up or spill something, all good fun.

Freddie played this part solidly for ten years – until many Variety theatres had closed down – that is, up to 1960. Then came a lean spell, during which his luck changed in amazing fashion.

With a wife and four children to support, Mr Frinton could not go on 'resting' (as being out of work is known in show business) indefinitely.

A decision was made to take over a business in Aldershot. Looking round the town he saw his friend Arthur Haynes billed at the Hippodrome, so he went back-stage to see him.

Haynes was delighted to see his old friend from *Stars in Battledress* and immediately offered Freddie a part in his forthcoming TV series. From then on, the Grimsby-born comedian went from success to success.

At Bradford in 1966 his well-known 'Dinner for One' sketch had been specially written into S H Newsome's comedy pantomime *Cinderella*.

That first weekend at pantomime rehearsal was where I saw him. On that occasion Freddie gave me some idea of how hectic an entertainer's life can be, and how gruelling the pace.

On the Saturday he had taken part in the final performance of Bernard Delfont's show *London Laughs* at the Palladium in London. Sunday saw him all day at the television studios, rehearsing and recording *Meet the Wife,* while on the Monday he had the long journey to Bradford, with a pantomime run-through at the end of it.

During the 32 weeks he was at the London Palladium Freddie Frinton became a grandfather. Proudly he showed me a newspaper cutting with a picture of the ceremony known as 'wetting the baby's head' in champagne.

In the picture were daughter Susan Moat with baby Sam (Samantha) together with Freddie and Thora. Grouped round were fellow Palladium stars Jimmy Tarbuck and Harry Secombe.

Freddie got a lot of fan mail. He showed me a suitcase full of letters.

'They send me pictures too' he said, holding up one which intrigued him very much. It had been sent to him by a lady admirer and bore the inscription: 'Cleethorpes, 1914'.

I examined it and saw that it depicted a concert party performing on the sands, the famous pier in the background. A notice on the platform-type stage gave the information that the pierrots perform 'Three times daily – At Eleven, Three and Seven O'clock – Weather and Tides permitting'.

'That's Fred Hughes's troupe at Cleethorpes, I reckon' said Freddie.

Then he added with a chuckle: 'But you won't find me on that one. It's a bit before my time!'

Sadly, I never saw him again…

GILLIN 1868-1942

'It walked...It talked...And it baffled everybody ...'

That was the description usually applied to 'Granfer' by the critics of the day. They were referring to the remarkable figure manipulated by 'Gillin – The Vent with Laughter Intent' – according to his bill matter.

The climax to the act came when the sprightly geriatric walked off into the wings of the theatre, still talking, quite independently of his mentor Gillin, who remained seated on a settee, centre stage.

Many rival 'vents' wanted to know 'how was it done?' but the mechanically minded Mr Gillin was not telling! Several stage critics referred to this remarkable phenomenon as 'a masterpiece of ingenuity' – which it undoubtedly was – the result being that Gillin invariably had a full date book.

Gillin – or William Edward Gillin – was a native of Clay Cross in Derbyshire, and from an early age had been interested in things mechanical. He began giving magic lantern displays at village halls around and about, and when cinematograph machines made their appearance in the 1890's, he was one of the first showmen to acquire one. Thus he was one of the pioneer northern operators who brought 'The Pictures to the People'.

It was whilst touring with his show in the 1900's that he met up with Will Onda, of the Onda Brothers, stage acrobats. They became great friends and associates. It was at this time Will Onda (real name Hugh Rain) was about to leave his partner and set up a film studio in his native Preston to make films and rent them out, as well as run a permanent cinema there.

Gillin was immediately interested, and when Onda, together with his son-in-law James Atroy (billed as 'The Society Juggler') began turning out pictures, Gillin began showing them. One well-paying venue was the Old Assembly Rooms in Rotherham, and for a time, the exhibitor made his home in that town.

The 'A1 Animated Pictures' were a great success and by 1908 'Film Seasons' were being given on a regular basis in halls in Barnsley and Doncaster.

One of the most successful films made by the A1 Film Company was a silent picture showing the renowned Dr Walford Bodie's stage act, which at that time comprised ventriloquism, mesmerism, and so-called 'electric wizardry'.

The 'vent' part of Bodie's act intrigued Gillin immensely. This was titled 'The Laird's Tea Party' (Bodie was a Scot) and in this scene the worthy Doctor presided over eight child figures, with himself at the head of the table.

Gillin's further interest in ventriloquism was stimulated by his sister-in-law's marriage to Coram, the Yorkshire-born vent. The result was that when Hewitt's, the brewers of Doncaster, decided to erect a Palace Theatre in that town, a new act was born. As there was Coram, so there would be Gillin, and an old bill of 1911 shows 'Gillin the Ventriloquist' billed over 'Palace Perfection Pictures'.

This was no co-incidence, for the 'A1 Animated Pictures' at the Corn Exchange ceased when the Palace opened, and Gillin moved his family to Doncaster forthwith – 'All Comms, to PA at 20 Buckingham Road'!

Then Hewitts decided to open another Palace in Scunthorpe. When this theatre opened at Easter, 1912, Gillin topped the bill. The vent was a top-line act!

At first, Gillin's act followed the style set by Dr Bodie of having several child figures on stage; then came the 'Granfer' speciality, and finally an act combining the best features of both.

The curtain would rise to reveal two child figures, a little boy and girl, seated either side of Gillin on a centre-stage settee. This act of 'Tommy and Nellie' caused 'gales of laughter wherever it appeared' according to a critic who saw the act many times. The latter describes a typical extract thus:-

Nellie begins to sing sweetly: 'Hark, I hear sweet music stealing round me...'

At this, Tommy interrupts with: 'What price rotten eggs today?'

Following this incident Tommy is put behind the couch 'in disgrace' but here he discovers a little dog – which causes more interruptions – until the act ends with Tommy crawling off stage pulling the little dog, which is on wheels!

Gillin's novelty act always went down well on the northern music halls, and always 'did a bomb' in Doncaster, but sadly the 'Pictures' which had seen the birth of the act, also brought about its demise.

Gillin found music halls being rapidly wired for 'talkies' and the venues for his act became fewer and fewer. Rather than play 'the clubs' he retired in 1933, but his unique stage act with Granfer, Tommy and Nellie, is still talked about today.

Jack GRAPHO 1906-1970

'I Say! I Say! I Say! Did you hear about the bookmaker's daughter?'
'The bookmaker's daughter? What about the bookmaker's daughter?'
'She came home at Twenty-to-One! Ha, ha, ha.'

The Jovial Jollies are in action on Saltburn Promenade in the 1930's.

Comedian Jack Grapho is engaged in 'verbal sparring' with Ernie Miller his 'feed', Tony Spoors is at the piano; La Tagarte 'The Famous Italian Baritone' gets ready to sing; Eva Walker, the soubrette, sits at the back of the open-air stage with the Deanella Girls (Marjorie, Jean and Elvira) who dance and add glamour to the show.

Corny stuff? But of course! Simplicity without smut was the keynote of success for the pierrot troupes and the Jovial Jollies were no exception. They did three shows a day – weather and tides permitting – and between times they all trouped off the promenade up the cliff walks to the big villa named Stanley House, where they all lived, on the Top Promenade.

Another Grapho gag was for Eva – or one of the girls – to mingle with the crowds which thronged the large iron shelter which faced the pierrot pitch and let out a piercing scream during his act. The point of this being that Jack had previously primed the punters in the deck chairs: 'I'll make you turn round in spite of yourselves – you see if I don't!'

Of course there was no inkling on that hot summer's day in 1939 that that particular season would be their last – Hitler's War saw to that – for hadn't there been a company of Grapho's Jovial Jollies in Saltburn since as far back as 1899?

'Established Forty Years' was a good recommendation indeed. They had tried other resorts – Withernsea and the Hartlepools for example – but they always came back to Saltburn, where they were 'favourites' and where it had all begun.

Mulvana's Minstrels, who had performed on the sands black-faced in the 'nineties, had contained three notable performers in Bert Grapho, comedian; Billy Jackson, pianist, and Little Phil (Phil Rees) vocalist.

When the Minstrels broke up, Grapho and Jackson formed the Jovial Jollies (a white-faced pierrot troupe), while Phil Rees got going with an act known as The Singing Stable Boys on the music halls. The latter recruited some notable performers in Dave Morris and Jimmy James.

Another venue with which the Grapho and Jackson troupe had happy associations was the Winter Gardens in the Abingdon Park at Northampton. Here, in 1909, a former roller skating rink was utilised as a pierrot pavilion, but it was always 'Saltburn for the Summer' where success was assured.

In later years the Jovial Jollies went on tour in the winter, and it was whilst their show was playing at Dumbarton in Scotland that Bert Grapho and his wife decided to adopt Wee Jack who was then nine years old and a promising performer.

Billy Jackson then having left the troupe, Bert Grapho put a revue on the Halls called *What a Lad!* starring Wee Jack, and this toured for years.

Bert Grapho was no mean performer himself. His speciality was lightning cartoons, and he was a particular favourite at the Stockton Hippodrome. When he died (about 1930) his widow carried on the Jovial Jollies at Saltburn.

Known as 'Mrs Bert' this little lady of the Halls was noted for wearing a fur coat, winter and summer, usually with a cloche hat. She had the able assistance of Jack, now grown up, and her 'right hand person' was Mary Martin. Mary had joined the company during the First War as a Scots comedienne and had stayed on to become 'Mrs Bert's' manager, and later companion, when the troupe packed up.

Jack Grapho, who was something of an institution in Saltburn and a great favourite with the kiddies, did a great deal of good work in the resort. Once he made the newspaper headlines by leaping over the safety fence and rescuing a small child from certain injury when it had strayed onto the track of the cliff tramway. He was presented with a gold watch for his bravery.

So well liked were the Jovial Jollies in Saltburn, that in the 1930's the Council allowed them to hold their Benefit Nights on the bandstand, in the wooded confines of Hazel Grove, where fairy lights twinkled in the trees and more deck chairs were placed at their disposal. All the performers got a 'benefit' in turn, but unfortunately the Council was powerless against the swarms of midges which assailed the onlookers on hot sunny nights, but it was all part of the fun.

After his adopted mother's death, Jack Grapho made his home in London, and reverted to his real name of McAlpine. Sadly his later years were marred by illness, but, great little trouper that he was, Wee Jack bore it all with a gag and a grin.

Jack Grapho certainly was a Lad...

Tommy HANDLEY 1894-1949

'Mother's pride and joy, Mrs Handley's boy,
It's useless to complain;
When trouble's brewing, it's his doing,
That Man – That Man again!'

Without doubt, the most successful radio series of all involving comedy was *ITMA* – or to give the full title – *It's That Man Again* which ran for nine years until the sad death of its 'anchor man' Tommy Handley.

In 1939 the BBC wanted a show to rival the popularity of the Askey-Murdoch vehicle *Band Wagon* and producer Francis Worsley came up with an idea for a series built round the fast-talking Liverpool comedian. Scripts were written by Francis Worsley and the first of six tentative broadcasts went out in July, 1939.

The show was a success from the start and made Tommy Handley a national figure.

Perhaps the secret was the host of odd characters that popped in and out to 'have a word with Mister Handley'.

To mention just a few, there was Jack Train who took the parts of Funf the Spy, and Colonel Chinstrap, with his catch-phrase 'I don't mind if I do!' Horace Percival, as Ali Oop, said 'I go, I coom back'. Dino Galvani as Signor So-So queried 'You called me, Meester Handle-pump?' Not forgetting Deryck Guyler (Frisby Dyke) and that man of many voices Fred Yule with Mark Time's 'I'll have to ask me Dad!'

Ladies in the show included a very young Hattie Jacques (as Sophie Tuckshop); Joan Harben (Mona Lott), and Dorothy Summers (as Mrs Mopp) had the listening audience in stitches with her entry line of 'Can I do you now, Sir?' and her exit tag 'Ta, Ta for now' which inevitably became 'TTFN'.

The central character in all this comic cacophony was a pioneer broadcaster, for Tommy had been 'on the air' since 1924, but a performer long before that.

The son of a Sefton Park dairyman, Reginald Thomas Handley left school in Liverpool at fifteen and began work at a toy-makers. Unimpressed, he then tried his luck at selling perambulators, but did not like that either.

Always stage struck as a youth, Tommy saw an advertisement in the *Liverpool Echo* which said that additional singers were required in the chorus, for the touring version of *The Maid of the Mountains,* apply the local Royal Court Theatre.

The year was 1911 and, having a pleasing baritone voice, Tommy passed the audition and so joined the company. Next to him in the line-up was an ex-Eton boy named Ronald Frankau and the pair struck up a friendship which lasted a lifetime.

Came the First War and the young Tommy Handley joined the Royal Naval Air Service. In 1917 he was stationed at Roehampton and in the same company was none other than George H Elliott – the 'Chocolate Coloured Coon' – from Rochdale!

Upon 'demob' it was back to work as a baritone for the Liverpool lad. In 1920 he joined a concert party at Bognor called The Sparklers. Charlie Harvey, the former Adeler and Sutton stalwart, was the comedian, and the pianist Jack Hylton.

In 1921, after further adventures, Hylton and Handley formed a vocal duo at the piano and got an engagement in Variety at the Bedford Palace in Camden Town.

The act was not a success so, while Jack Hylton gave his attention to dance bands, Tommy Handley (at the instigation of Leslie Henson) took a part in a sketch about to tour titled 'The Disorderly Room'. Tommy took the part of the officer.

Described as 'a sketch set to music of the twenties', and written by Eric Blore, 'The Disorderly Room' was extra-ordinarily successful. With frequent revivals, Tommy toured it for twenty years – from 1921 to 1941 – and it went into the Royal Variety Performance of 1924 held at the London Coliseum, which was broacast 'live'.

Tommy came over the air waves very well and was given a part in the very first wireless revue titled *Radio Radiance* in 1925. This proved to be 'Radio Romance' for Mr Handley, for in this was showgirl Jean Allistone who became his wife.

Our man's career was now destined for broadcasting, for he was chosen to compere the Royal Variety Performance of 1927 from the Victoria Palace. He also shared with Leonard Henry what have been described as 'the popularity polls of the Savoy Hill days!

In 1930 he met up again with Ronald Frankau, who had been broadcasting since 1927, and they did a *North and South* programme. In 1934 they did a series *Murgatroyd and Winterbottom,* Tommy being the latter. While other comedy duos were leisurely, Frankau and Handley delivered their puns and gags at high speed – as fast funsters!

So when *ITMA* came into being, fast-talking Tommy was a natural choice.

One can only speculate what would have happened if *ITMA* had made the transition to television. But the show was built round Tommy Handley and could not go on without him.

Will HAY 1888-1949

'Good Morning, Boys!'
'Good Morning, Sir'
'Let us commence lessons with a will'
'Why? Are you going to make yours?'

Such was the back-chat Will Hay had to put up
with from his pupils in his famous schoolmaster
stage speciality 'The Fourth Form at St Michaels'
which toured the music halls for many years.

William Thompson Hay thought of becoming an engineer – in fact, became an apprentice – but instead became a performer at local concerts, reciting and singing. It was a good thing for the British Variety stage that he did – and the film industry – for Will Hay became the most original and enduring film comedian produced by these islands in the 1930's.

In his early days he was encouraged by his schoolteacher sister, who gave him ideas for his material. In fact it was a song she wrote for him about a headmaster that gave Will the idea for Dr Smart Allick and the unruly pupils in the famous sketch, with himself as Head.

After a try-out with Buxton's Pierrots in the Isle of Man, Will Hay joined Fred Karno's famous repertory company of comedians in 1909. He stayed with the Master of Slapstick for two years, gaining valuable experience in the art of making people laugh.

Hay's first professional appearance on the stage was with Karno in Manchester in 1909, and he reached London two years later, with an appearance at the old Surrey Theatre, where he was to become a particular favourite.

At this time he was billed as 'The Eccentric Comedian' but in 1912 his sister Elspeth wrote him *The Bend Down Song* – which went with a 'swish' and a warning to all naughty boys – and so, garbed in gown and mortar-board, the famous schoolmaster character eventually emerged.

In his years on the Halls with himself as the Head of St Michaels, his stooge pupils were his nephews, Bert and Cyril Platt, but later on the idea was developed with his son, Will Hay Jnr and Gordon Saunders. Later still, with the screen version, there were changes again.

Will's famous 'Fourth Form at St Michael's' sketch went down well in the Royal Variety Performance of 1930 at the London Hippodrome, and it was this success that led to Dr Smart Allick and his Pupils being transferred to the screen five years later, when *Boys Will Be Boys* was made.

Then in 1938 came *Oh! Mr Porter,* which has been described as the 'funniest British picture ever made', *The Ghost of St Michaels* in 1941 and finally *The Goose Steps Out* made in 1942, which gave a film start to Barry Morse and Peter Ustinov.

Will Hay's success on the silver screen was well summed up by John Huntley, formerly of the British Film Institute, as follows:- 'Will Hay did not look like a comedian. He had a plain, ordinary, cross sort of a face, a marked speech defect, and a regular air of puzzled irritation.

'He always portrayed figures of authority – schoolmasters, policemen, station masters, prison governors – to whom he imparted an air of seediness and corruption.

'If he was not beset by a school of unruly and generally aged boys, he was teamed with Moore Marriott and Graham Moffatt, respectively a capering, sly, whiskery, senile old idiot called Harbottle, and a gross and idle youth of the Dickensian mould, who answered to Albert'.

Hay, who liked to study astrology in his spare time (he is reported to have charted a spot on Saturn!), died after a long illness. Besides his son, Will Hay Jnr, his daughter Gladys Hay also had a stage career, and is well remembered for her comedy role in the radio show *Ignorance is Bliss.*

No one seems to know who first put it about that Will Hay was born in Aberdeen. He wasn't. He was born in a little terraced house in Stockton-on-Tees – at 23 Durham Street to be precise – and Mary Edwards of the Teesside Film Theatre some years ago obtained a copy of his birth certificate to prove it. This records that Will was born there 6th December, 1888.

Too bad this fact was not established sooner. That little house should have been saved for posterity. But 'too late' is the cry! The populace is wise after the event. The bulldozers have been, gone, and left nothing...

Dick HENDERSON 1891-1958

A well-remembered figure in the hey-day of the music halls was genial Dick Henderson, father of Dickie. A fat little man in a bowler hat, puffing an equally fat cigar, he had a pungent line in patter.

Dick always made his entrance and exit to the strains of *Tiptoe Through the Tulips* and managed a step-dance to boot.

Born on North Humberside, in a little house in Strawberry Street at Drypool, Dick began his working life as an apprentice fitter at Earle's Shipyard in Hull. In his spare time he began 'obliging with a turn' in the pubs and clubs of Hull's dock-land, in particular the old Andrew Marvel in the Hessle Road.

One summer he left the shipyard and joined the pierrots at Withernsea. He got £2 and a share of the 'bottle' and was highly delighted. Audiences liked his jokes and he began to think about a career in entertainment.

That winter he signed forms for Hull Kingston Rovers, to play as a prop forward, but left Craven Park abruptly when an agent offered him a part in touring revue as a comedian, salary £4 10s a week. Dick jumped at this opportunity. His first London appearance was at the old Canning Town Imperial Theatre in 1914.

Came the First War and the young Henderson joined the Navy as a cook, but was soon back on dry land after being torpedoed. There is a story that he sang to the lads when the SS Rievaulx Abbey went down. (In later years a fellow performer, Will Wise, said that Dick could always rustle up some grub if need be, adding that Dick could always fall back on being a chef if things got really bad!)

Discharged from the Navy in 1918, Dick went to America to try his luck on the stage in that great country. He married there after a whirlwind courtship. Then he toured the United States as a performer in Vaudeville and made motion pictures for Warner Brothers.

Returning to this country in the 1920's he was honoured by a spot in the Royal Variety Performance of 1926, where he scored a great success. Then he made several tours, both of this country and abroad, perfecting his comedy act in the process.

In later life the comedian joined Don Ross's famous Thanks For The Memory company of veteran performers and did several successful tours with them. He received a tumultous reception when he appeared in his native city Hull, with this show, at the Palace Theatre there in 1957.

Billed as 'The Yorkshire Comedian' the rotund comic with the big cigar proved he had lost none of his native dialect with his sojurn in the States. His verbal asides and pungent patter were as direct and funny as ever.

A year later Dick Henderson died suddenly only a few days before he was due to appear in what would have been his third Royal Variety show. Shortly before this he had had to withdraw from a show called Large as Life at the London Palladium.

If sadly Dick Henderson did not live to appear in his third Royal Variety Performance, he was proud that his son Dickie followed him into the profession that was so dear to his heart.

In a tribute to Dick's memory, R B Marriott, critic of The Stage newspaper wrote: 'Dick Henderson's stories and comments usually concerned suburban life – the 'subbubs' as he said. What he did not tell us about certain aspects of mothers-in-law, sweethearts, marriage and a score of other familiarities of everyday life, was probably not worth hearing.

'His range may have been limited, but it went to the very heart and spirit of the matter; and the matter was concerned with the ironical side of life, which he brought before us so vividly.

'He could sing a sweet ballad very well indeed, but what joyous comedy there was in his acid comments on the disenchantments of domesticity!

'If only Dick Henderson's stories and verbal asides could have been collected...'

If only they could indeed.

Leonard HENRY 1891-1973

'I Say! I Say! I Say! Do you like my tit-fer? A bit of alright – don't-cher-think?
Now, can I have my umbrella please? Thanks – Ooh... The other way round – If you don't mind...'

'A true-blue Cockney with an infectious brand of humour' was the description applied by one critic to Leonard Henry, concert party artiste turned broadcaster, in BBC radio programmes of yester-year.

In those far off pre-television days of 2LO, his peculiar 'babbling style of delivery' (as described by another critic) endeared itself to a large number of listeners. The man from Kennington Oval was certainly popular.

Born Leonard H Ruming, the son of Harry Ruming, concert party promoter, Henry claimed to be the only comedian to 'go on the stage with a bang'. Perhaps it would be more correct to say that he went on stage as the result of one!

The said explosion occured at the chemical factory where he had commenced work in the office, after completing his education at Alleyn's School, his father being determined that his son follow a commercial career.

However, it was not to be. Leonard went to Southend to recuperate, and it was at this resort his father ran The Mountebanks concert party. Before long he was 'helping out at the piano' (ostensibly to pass the time) but before long he had persuaded his father to take him on as the troupe's regular pianist.

Leonard Henry liked concert party work. He was convinced the open air life was for him. In a letter to Clarkson Rose he wrote: 'What fun and high adventure it all was! How we took everything in our stride – the collection box, parts in laughable sketches – and even taking the piano off the stage and up the hill side, where the audience preferred to sit in hot weather.

'In short, if the people would not come to us, we would go to them...'

'There were three shows a day – at eleven, three, and eight o'clock – salary one pound, ten shillings. And one managed to save!'

In this way Leonard Henry joined the pierrots. Soon afterwards he scored a great success at the Winter Gardens in Margate during 1912, where he added songs and patter to his piano act. And so the ex-chemist began dispensing humour!

In the 1920's he had graduated to Charlot's Revues and played opposite lovely Phyllis Monkman (of Co-optimists fame) in a show at the Prince of Wales' Theatre in the West End. He crowned his stage career with a Royal Variety Performance at the London Palladium in 1952.

However, it was on sound radio he scored his greatest success, the microphone being adjusted to his height of 'precisely five feet' to give him 'maximum impact on the air waves'. The little comedian wrote all his own material, and fed the microphone 'a constant stream of radio-active patter' which went down very well with listeners.

He gave listeners the impression that he simply prattled and sang about anything that came into his head as he went along, but in point of fact all his material was very carefully prepared and rehearsed. Topical gags were a speciality of his, and he read the morning papers assiduously to 'keep his patter pungent'.

Leonard Henry went to the Alexandra Palace ('Ally-Pally') to take part in some very early television transmissions in the 1930's, but soon returned to his 'old love' of sound radio when war broke out, and the BBC moved to Bristol for a time in the 1940's.

Henry's hobbies were cats and cars, and it seems he possessed a weird collection of umbrellas, of which he was very proud. However, his main interest was without doubt work, and he was engaged on the writing of new scripts and patter till the end.

Someone once asked him the secret of his success.

He replied, with typical Henry humour: 'I owe everything to my creditors!'

Sydney HOWARD 1883-1946

'What's to do?' was the catch-phrase of Sydney Howard, concert party comic turned film actor.

Syd, of the fluttering fingers and portly figure, took the phrase with him into pictures, where he portrayed butlers, tipsy photographers, and other simple types with the greatest of ease.

Beginning his working life as a traveller for his Uncle's printing firm, the young Howard became an enthusiastic member of the local amateurs, who put on shows in Yeadon, his native town in Yorkshire.

With the amateurs – known in Yeadon as 'The Hammer Chewers' – he became a well-known figure at their venue 'T'Peeps in Football' (The Peoples' Hall in the Football Field) and was a gradely choice as Buttons in *Cinderella,* a pantomime staged there early in the century. (It was in this particular pantomime that shapely Nell Houghton as the Prince shocked the natives by daring to appear in tights!)

One day in the summer of 1911 there was consternation in the wood and canvas concert party pavilion at Undercliffe, near Bradford. This was when the leading comedian of Scott Barrie's Chanticleers was suddenly taken ill and could not appear. The urgent problem of a substitute was solved when someone thought 'that slow-witted droll from Yeadon' might be available.

The said droll was sent for, substituted, and 'went over big' although he was not even billed to appear! Sydney did his speciality – a recitation called *Paper Bag Cookery* and cracked a few simple gags – and this success prompted him to turn professional, as a comedian.

He left the printers and for the 1912 season was engaged by Freddy Carlton (Cousin Freddy) who ran the White Coons at St Annes-on-sea. In the company was a former grave digger from Bolton – a handsome fair-haired fellow named Terry Wilson – and the two became firm friends. Terry Wilson was a light comedian and in later years became a 'fixture' in the Blackpool entertainment scene, where he earned the nick-name of 'Mr Squires Gate'.

After further experience with Fred Walmsley's Tonics in Blackpool, Sydney Howard went on tour with the famous Splinters company, which contained another friend of his in the person of Jimmy Slater. Jimmy was a wonderful female impersonator, whose parents kept the Albert Hotel back in Yeadon.

Following the Splinters success, Jimmy Slater ran concert parties at Cleethorpes and other places, while Syd Howard, after experience with a revue called *The Radium Girls,* went into musical comedy in the West End. One success in particular was *Box O' Tricks* which ran for a time at the London Hippodrome.

Later Howard went into British films, and in the 1930's migrated to Hollywood, but returned to this country to make more pictures. He made some twenty films in all, including the *Splinters* series, *Tilly of Bloomsbury, Shipyard Sally,* to name but a few. One of his finest roles was as the tipsy photographer in J B Priestley's *When We Are Married* which was transferred from stage to the screen.

The Yeadon born comedian made so much money from pictures that in later life he was able to live it up in style in the South of France.

'The wife's health, you know' he would say, adding: 'Of course, I like Blackpool best!' No doubt this latter observation was made to sustain the image of the North Country man of simple tastes he so liked to portray.

Sydney Howard played stage and screen drunks with ease, but never touched a drop himself. He was a life-long Methodist and teetotaller, and put this down to early attendance at Queen Street Chapel in Yeadon.

The comedian claimed his success with drunk portrayals was brought about by studying the antics of inebriates in public houses which he visited as a young man – he was a 'regular' at the Albert Hotel in Yeadon, kept by his friends, the Slaters – but he only drank ginger beer.

Perhaps Sydney Howard is best remembered as the simple Yorkshire Tyke in the huge scarf, supporting his local soccer team at Wembley, in *Up For The Cup,* part of which was filmed in Yeadon.

The 'Slow-witted droll from Yeadon' scored a great goal with this shooting...

Jimmy JAMES 1892-1965

'Are you putting it about that I'm barmy?'

A tall, weedy, open-mouthed character is speaking. Wearing a deerstalker hat, a shrunken suit with trousers at half-mast, Bretton Woods demands an answer.

Not far away ashen-faced Hutton Conyers, in ankle-length overcoat, gazes vacantly at the ceiling.

Between them, top-hatted Jimmy James, unsteady on his feet and with dress scarf flailing about, fingers a broken cigarrete, then slurs out the reply: 'Why, are you keeping it a secret?'

It is June, 1958 and the Joseph family are putting on *The Greatest Show of All* at the famous Leeds City Varieties. Needless to say, the line-up includes Jimmy James and Company.

Jimmy James, the stage 'drunk' with the cigarette prop, was complete master of the ad-lib. His timing was superb. Gags came in a never ending stream from his lips, to bounce back from his stooges with the belligerancy of billiard balls.

James hailed these stooges as his 'discoveries'. One he swore was 'The Singing Werewolf'. The other he said was the greatest find since sliced bread. Both were named after unusual places: Bretton Woods after a war-time conference; Hutton Conyers after a village near Ripon Racecourse.

Many top-line comedians acknowledge they owe a lot to Jimmy. Roy Castle became one of his stooges in the 1950's 'to gain experience'. What finer tribute could there be to the man than that? Peter Sellers, Frankie Howard and Bruce Forsyth studied him in action at any and every opportunity.

When he was taken ill, impresario Bernard Delfont arranged for the biggest 'Benefit' ever known for a performer in show business.

Delfont donated his 1,000-seat Prince of Wales' Theatre in the West End for a *Sunday Night with the Stars* show. The cast, which included Frankie Howerd, Bruce Forsyth, Roy Castle, Max Bygraves, Janette Scott, Millicent Martin and Diana Dors, would have done credit to a Royal Variety Performance. The place was packed.

All these Stars (and many more) bent their expensive schedules to appear in this tribute. Script-writers Simpson and Galton worked for free. Bed-ridden Jimmy James was touched by the gesture.

This true 'King of the Ad-Lib' was born James Casey in Portrack Lane, Stockton-on-Tees, the son of a steel worker. As a boy little Jimmy clog-danced for coppers outside his terraced home. At twelve he won a talent competition at Middlesbrough.

Then Phil Rees, who ran a juvenile troupe called The Stable Boys, came to the Stockton Hippodrome. Little Jimmy joined them as 'Terry Casey – The Blue-eyed Boy'. His speciality? A standing jump over a five-barred gate.

After touring for years with Phil Rees, and then Will Netta's company (doing step-dancing and singing) came the First War, which saw him join the Northumberland Fusiliers. He was gassed, so he could not go back to singing. Instead he joined Tom Convery's stable of comedians.

His big chance came in 1925 when on tour. Comic Jimmy Basso walked out of the show at the Longton Regent, and James Casey replaced him, billed as Jimmy James. He got £12 a week – good money then – and decided to keep the name.

Then Dick Batch, the Wallasey script-writer, wrote him a sketch called 'The Spare Room' which went over well. So the Drunk act was born, improved later by the addition of stooges and the opening music of *Three O'Clock in the Morning.*

Strangely enough Jimmy James, who made the perfect drunk, never touched the stuff himself. But he did like to gamble. Once, during a season at Blackpool, he went for a haircut every day. Jimmy discovered that the barber also took bets!

This weakness with money led to several 'confrontations' with the Tax people and the Official Receiver. In the middle of his act at the Lewisham Hippodrome in 1939 he saw two tipstaffs waiting in the wings. Turning to his stooges, he announced: 'Those men have come to measure me for my gas mask!'

The Teesside comedian earned his title 'King of the Ad-Libbers' for his spontaneous and un-rehearsed humour. Once, in the middle of a sketch, he turned to Bretton Woods and said: 'Did you put this Government in?'

When the stooge protested, Jimmy said: 'Well, someone like you did!'

But the real gem of the lot came when he was playing the Crown Theatre at Eccles during the height of the 'blitz'. When Jimmy James and Company were on stage, a land-mine fell nearby and blew open every door in the theatre.

Quite unconcernedly, Mr James knocked the ash off his cigarette and said:

'It's that wedding party at the back again. They're far too noisy. Will someone tell them either to keep quiet or get out!'

Joe KING 1900-1967

'Do you like me shirt? It's not me best one. Ah lent that to a feller an' he wearn't return it'.
'When Ah asked him why, he said: 'Ay, lad. Ah can't. Ah laid me Dad out in it...'

Joe King is on stage at the Halifax Palace. A dapper little man in a grey suit, red tie and bowler hat. He wears 'Manhattans' and puts one foot on the footlights as he talks. As he exchanges banter with MD Vic Lewis, he leans over the orchestra pit and knocks the ash from his cigarette down amongst the musicians.

Very important to Joe is the cigarette. He times his act with it. After coming on stage to the strains of *Colonel Bogey* (played with gusto by the said musicians) he lights his fag. He knows when it burns away his time is up. He then exits to a comic song: *Our House has the Mucky Curtains* – 'The last one down the left hand side...'

The King comedian had a particular affinity with the Halifax Palace, known as 'Britain's sweetest theatre', for he began his stage career there in 1937 and took his last bow on its boards twenty years later.

The Palace was called 'Britain's sweetest theatre' because, when they built it in 1902, the cement would not set, so they mixed sugar with it!

When the management of the MacNaghten circuit decided that Variety was finished at the Palace in 1957, Joe decided to call it a day also, and retire from the stage.

Joe King – always joking – was no relation to Nosmo King (as he often pointed out) but he got his stage name in a similar manner.

Whereas Nosmo King (Vernon Watson) saw 'No Smoking' on some scene dock doors and appropriated the idea, Joe King (Cecil Emmott) got his name from a neighbour – a gas man in Glusburn, Yorkshire, whose real name it was. (In Glusburn, Joe was always known as Our Cecil, pronounced Cee-cil, by the way).

At that time, in the 1930's, Our Cecil was 'on the buses'. That is, he drove the Skiptonian between Cross Hills and Skipton, and also 'had a go' at driving the red buses in Keighley, when they scrapped the 'tracklesses' (trolley-buses to you). He was also a 'club turn', and a very good one, too. (Someone said: 'Why don't you go on the stage?' and so he did.)

After a 'trial turn' at Halifax Palace, an agent got him a booking at the old Argyle Theatre in Birkenhead – where he impressed Danny Clarke – so Joe King was soon on his way. It was not long before Francis Laidler booked him for the Keighley Hippodrome, where the natives saw him, and immediately recognised him as Our Cecil – one time programme boy!

Unlike many of the northern comedians – who 'died the death' south of Birmingham – Joe King went over very well down South. In fact, he played the London Palladium for George Black and the Victoria Palace for Jack Hylton.

Joe gagged about this, saying 'I'm the only comic who's gone from the Victoria Pub (in Keighley) to the Victoria Palace (in London) and survived!'

In connection with the Keighley comedian's first appearance at the Victoria Palace, there is a story, which runs as follows. When a local taxi driver named Horsfall heard of the booking, he was so excited for Joe that he offered to drive him to London and back for £3. Joe jumped at the offer, only to learn that he was expected to find the driver digs for the week he was in London!

A great pal of Joe's was the Irish tenor, Josef Locke, and the pair appeared together in many shows at the old Feldman's Theatre in Blackpool, the Isle of Man, and elsewhere. They were a familiar sight driving about Blackpool in a Daimler car.

Arthur Haynes was a great admirer of the Glusburn comedian's style, and finally acquired some of his gag books. Most of these were written by his wife's sister, Our Teresa.

Joe King's particular style of humour registered very well 'on the wireless' and the comedian made many broadcasts from the old North Regional Station. He appeared in *Worker's Playtime* during the War and broadcast so many times from Steeton Dump (the RO Factory) that people thought he must work there!

At one period his daughter Eileen was co-opted to join the act – as his stage wife – and she made an admirable 'feed'. In this connection a recording in the series *Blackpool Nights* is well remembered, especially a scene 'Domestic Bliss'.

The neglected wife says reproachfully: 'You promised to love me all my life'.

'I know' said Joe. 'But I never thought you'd live so long!'

Nosmo **KING** 1886-1949

Vernon Watson was a popular Variety artiste, touring the music halls before and after the First War, but he never rose above the level of the 'wines and spirits' in regard to bill matter. Some years later an event occured which was to change all that.

A former Liverpool bank clerk, H Vernon Watson very clearly showed a leaning towards things theatrical, and soon joined the local amateur dramatic society. There he gained valuable stage experience, and it was soon evident that he had a rare talent for mimicry.

In 1911 he turned professional, using his real name of Vernon Watson, doing impressions of the leading comedians of the day. These included Albert Chevalier, Fred Emney Snr, and George Robey. These were good enough to obtain him bookings at London halls and a part in a revue titled *By George!*

Then, when Frank Tinney, the American black-faced comedian (who had caused such a sensation at the New York Winter Garden in 1912) came to this country, Vernon Watson added an impression of him to his repertoire. As this was a 'black-face' study, Watson always closed his act with this number, often using it as an encore – giving him time to apply the make-up.

He noticed that this impression gained him great applause, and when Frank Tinney returned to his native America, Watson gave thought to a different style of act based upon a black-face personality.

Opportunity for this came about in the early 1920's when the manager of the music hall at which he was appearing requested him to do a 'second spot' later in the programme, for a performer who had not put in an appearance.

Watson had the black-face study ready, but was stuck for a name. Then inspiration came to his aid. The scene dock doors were partly open, back-stage at the theatre, and the two halves read 'No Smo king'. That was it. From then on, the black-face character would be Nosmo King!

Very soon Vernon Watson found that the second spot as Nosmo King went over with audiences a whole lot better than the character impressions under his own name. Accordingly, the Nosmo King personality was developed and finally the stage act of 'Nosmo King and Hubert' was billed in 1925 and onwards, when his son Jack Watson joined him in the act. At this, Vernon Watson made his last bow.

The act of Nosmo King and Hubert consisted of the former dressed in a red flunkey's livery, with a black face, white-rimmed glasses and smoking a cigar. Hubert occupied the musical director's chair during his father's act, and the pair exchanged banter.

Another feature of the act was the closing monologue, by Nosmo. For a long time this was *The Touch of a Master's Hand* inspired by the memory of an old violinist, but later on came a series of popular patriotic monologues.

This came about during the Second War, when Nosmo King went solo, the reason being that Hubert joined-up! The son became Petty Officer Jack Watson of the Royal Navy, and he occasionally made appearances and broadcasts, Naval duties permitting. (Later on he became a character actor in his own right).

'The end' came for Nosmo King early in 1949, when he died in his sleep in his Chelsea flat. He had been greatly upset by the sudden death of his old friend from Liverpool, Tommy Handley, and this seemed to un-nerve him. However, he had continued to act as Chairman in the radio series *Palace of Varieties* with great success, the monologues in particular being in great demand.

In regard to Frank Tinney: since his return to America he had been unable to recapture that peculiar 'gregarious intimacy with his audience' for which his critics gave him credit. He died in comparative obscurity, except for one thing which gained him immortality. This was when Charlie Chaplin saw him – and hardly recognised him as the same man – the result being that Chaplin wrote the film script of *Limelight* and based the character of Calvero upon him. (Calvero was the broken-down old performer, played in the film by Chaplin.)

Back to Nosmo King: During an interview the Liverpool comedian made two remarkable confessions. The first one was that someone had pointed out to him that a cigar smoking figure was hardly compatible with the name 'Nosmo King' and suggested he gave up the weed. This he found remarkably difficult, but he eventually accomplished it with the aid of snuff.

The second confession was that he had never at any time, set eyes on Frank Tinney!

Harry KORRIS 1888-1971

'We three... In Happidrome, Just a set of twirps maybe; Ramsbottom, and Enoch, and Me...'

So sang Harry Korris, otherwise 'Mr Lovejoy', in company with Ramsbottom (Cecil Frederick) and Enoch (Robbie Vincent) in the radio and stage show *Happidrome* which ran – on and off – between 1941 and 1947.

Known as 'The Falstaff of the South Pier'

during the eleven years he played in summer seasons at Blackpool, comedian Harry Korris was a great favourite with holiday audiences. He appeared in Ernest Binns' *Arcadian Follies* and the show did more than fifty broadcasts from the old North Regional Station.

At Whitsuntide, 1939, Mr Korris said he had received six offers to make films, which he had to refuse, the reason being that 'he was booked solid until the end of 1940'. Of course, the War changed all that, the result being that he went into *Happidrome*.

This was the best thing he ever did, for the show was a hit from the start.

The original trio included Albert Modley and Max Norris, but for the highly successful BBC sound version the formula was changed to include Cecil Frederick as Ramsbottom, Robbie Vincent as Enoch, and Harry Korris as Mr Lovejoy.

However, in spite of *Happidrome*, Harry found time to make three films with Wigan-born comic Frank Randle, in which all the stooges took part. These were made on a shoe-string budget by the Blakeley-inspired Mancunian Films (at The Parsonage in Manchester) and titles included *Somewhere in England, Somewhere in Camp* and *Somewhere in Civvies.* In 1943 a film version was made of *Happidrome*.

A great pierrot and comedian, Harry was born Henry L Corris at Douglas, in the Isle of Man. He made his stage debut as a pierrot at the Onchan Head Pavilion in 1906 but three years later the great Fred Buxton switched him to the Villa Marina, a much better venue.

His fame as a Pierrot comedian spread and Will Ambro who ran *The Debonairs* brought him to the mainland in 1913 to appear in pantomime at the old Queens' Palace in Shipley and a summer season at the Lidget Green Pavilion, near Bradford.

During the First War these pierrot pavilions had to close down, and Harry Korris was booked for touring revue, where he met his wife Connie Emerson, who had appeared as soubrette with Bert Grapho's Jovial Jollies at Hartlepool.

According to Lily Austin, the revue that brought Harry fame was *Gay Paree,* formerly toured by the Sunderland-born comedian Mark Sheridan.

When Sheridan died tragically in 1917, impresario William Revill bought the show intact from his widow and, with Harry Korris as comedian and Lily Austin 'The Yorkshire Nightingale' as the star turn, the show toured for four years.

1921 saw Harry Korris back again at Lidget Green, this time in Ernest Binns' *Merrie Arcadians,* a show which contained Fred Walker, the father of comedian Freddie Sales. This was the beginning of Harry's long association with Mr Binns.

The Second War brought *Happidrome* in which Harry had the services of another Harry – Harry Mitchel-Craig – who became his manager and script compiler.

When this run finally ended in 1947, Mr Korris toured with Elva Sheridan as his stage partner in *Mr Lovejoy Goes to Paris.* When this finally came off the road at Barnsley Theatre Royal in 1950, Harry took things easy in Blackpool.

But it is for his radio comedy the Isle of Man comedian is best remembered, in particular his many appearances in *Happidrome.* In banter with Robbie ('Let Me Tell You') Vincent, Harry used to say: 'I'll tell him! Where's Enoch?'

At this, pallid-faced Enoch would shuffle on and announce: 'Let me tell you, Mr Lovejoy, my teacher says I'm a soldier of heaven'. Harry would groan at this, and reply: 'Well, tell your teacher you're a hell of a long way from your barracks!'

Cecil Frederick, who had been with Korris since 1926, was also a superb 'foil'.

Harry got a lot of fan mail from these *Happidrome* broadcasts and one letter he mentioned gave him a lot of pleasure. It was from an old lady living at South Shore in Blackpool and read as follows: 'Dear Mr Korris, Will you please tell your artistes to sing a little louder in Friday's broadcast, as my radio set's batteries are running down.'

Jack LANE 1879·1953

Audiences at the famous Leeds City Varieties are used to unusual acts, but at Whitsuntide, 1911 even they were astonished at the ability displayed on that occasion by Jack Lane, billed as 'The Yorkshire Rustic'.

This performer during the course of his act sat down at the piano; played *Cock O' the North* with one hand, his signature tune *Hello!* with the other, and at the same time sang *On Ilkla' Moor Baht 'At* (The Yorkshireman's 'anthem') to a different tune altogether!

Even worthy Fred Wood (owner of the Varieties at the time) and J C 'Tich' Whiteman (manager) were impressed by that feat. And for Jack Lane himself it was the realisation of an ambition – to top the bill at a music hall – which he certainly did on that occasion – and many times afterwards.

Jack was not a native of Leeds, but a Halifax lad, real name John Edward Rider. However, he made so many appearances among the 'wines and spirits' (as a supporting act) at the old Queen's Palace in Jack Lane, Holbeck – which is a suburb of Leeds – that he decided to adopt the thoroughfare of that theatre as a stage name!

His act was certainly versatile. It was part musical – both vocal and instrumental – as well as embodying dialect studies, patter and comedy.

The son of a Halifax shoe-maker, Jack always said he got his musical ability from his mother, who 'put him to the piano at an early age' and saw that he got plenty of practice.

The lad from Savile Park began his working life as an engineer in Halifax, but having completed his apprenticeship was promptly paid off, to his great delight, as he 'hated the job'.

His mother found him a job as an analyst, but he did not stick that long, being more interested in music. He soon found himself singing and playing in the public houses and singing rooms of his native town.

Jack was also interested in early gramophones – known then as 'phono-graphs' – and put his engineering training to good use by making himself a machine which played cylinders and records. During his holidays he took this machine to Blackpool and played popular records of the day for visitors, from a pitch on the sands, for coppers. The Edison Bell Company heard of this enterprise and objected strongly.

When they saw his machine, they promptly took possession of it. Apparently it was much better than the model they were marketing – embodying many more features – and gave him one of theirs! After that he claimed to be an 'Official Phonograph Operator'!

Jack Lane's first appearance on the music hall stage was in his native Halifax, at the Oddfellow's Hall, also known as 'The People's Palace' in 1902. This was when he was pressed into service to accompany Leo Dryden (who sang his famous ditty written by Will Godwin *The Miner's Dream of Home)* when a pianist was required.

Later in that same year of 1902 he assisted the great Houdini – both musically and mechanically – when the escapologist paid his first visit to Halifax.

An agent saw Jack performing and, recognising his ability, offered him a pantomime engagement in Doncaster at £5 a week. At this, the man from Savile Park stopped 'analysing' and decided to make the music hall stage his career.

When the Doncaster engagement led to a tour of South Africa, he decided to get married on the strength of it. As the pro's say, he 'never looked back' and topping the bill at Leeds was simply proof that he had 'arrived'.

Jack Lane was a great favourite in pantomime, making many appearances in his favourite roles of Simple Simon and Idle Jack. He also made many friends in the profession, two in particular being Wilkie Bard and Rochdale-born G H Elliott.

The comedy part of his act was so good that he unwittingly cured a shell-shocked soldier in 1916. The soldier, rendered dumb by gunfire, was sitting in the audience at the Sunderland Empire and laughed so much at Lane's act that he got his voice back. The soldier leaped to his feet in the stalls, shouting: 'Bravo! I can speak. Bravo, Jack!'

In later years Jack Lane made a name for himself on sound radio. He appeared in *Variety Bandbox* and *Palace of Varieties* with great success. He also had a hand in 'discovering' the great comedienne Tessie O'Shea, in so much as he wrote songs and patter for her, in her early stage career.

'The Yorkshire Rustic' did not quite do fifty years on stage. After forty-nine he decided to take things easy, and study 'fowk' as in his dialect studies…

Jimmy **LEARMOUTH** 1891-1921

'Does a man in a fur coat eat pork pies?'

A moustached figure in a moth-eaten fur coat and battered straw hat bounds onto the stage and points at the audience.

Thus Jimmy Learmouth makes his entrance and convulses the customers. Years later Bud Flanagan adopts the same gear and gets the same laughs.

Gateshead-born comedian Jimmy Learmouth began and ended his stage career in the same town – Sheffield – and at the same theatre.

First employed by Joe Peterman in a supporting role in sketches, Jimmy's big chance came in classical fashion when the comedian of the show refused to appear one night at the Sheffield Empire. Young Learmouth stepped in at a moment's notice and did well. He kept the part and never looked back. Very soon he went solo.

Although his career as a top comedian was short – spanning less than a decade – it was one of outstanding success.

From an early age he was addicted to a fatal weakness of funny men – drink.

According to an old lady who lived in Eastern Street at Gateshead, even before he became a star, Jimmy drank a great deal. She recalls that the noise from the Learmouth house on a Saturday night could be heard all over the street.

After a collapse and being carried off at the nearby Newcastle Hippodrome, Jimmy recovered, and insisted upon appearing in pantomime at Sheffield. This was as Buttons in *Cinderella* at the Empire, for impresario Julian Wylie, the season 1920/21.

But the strain proved too much, and a few short months later, the thirty-year-old Learmouth – who was billed as 'The Comic Whose Smile Never Wears Off' – died in a nursing home at Broadstone in Dorset.

Very little has been written about Jimmy Learmouth, but he is well remembered by the novelist J B Priestley, who first saw the comedian in a sketch at the Bradford Empire before the First War (Harry Day's revue *Keep To The Right),* and again during that war, at a camp theatre in North Wales.

Mr Priestley's recollections of Jimmy Learmouth were broadcast in March, 1972 from BBC Newcastle, in a programme entitled *The Great North Road Show,* and his comments make interesting reading.

In answer to the question: 'What do you remember about Jimmy Learmouth?' Mr Priestley replied: 'Well, let me say to begin with, how glad I am for the chance of talking about him, for he was one of the best comedians I ever saw, and I am an authority on these things, I really am. I have studied them, I have written about them, and I am a kind of comedian myself, in a very dignified fashion.

'I first saw Learmouth before the First War. He was touring then in long and rather elaborate sketches, and he was very, very funny. But he was better still during the War, when, after I had been to France and had been wounded and so on, I went in 1917 to Kinmel Park Camp, near Rhyl.

'There, to my great joy, they had a camp theatre, and they alternated between straight theatre and a sort of Variety and Revue. Jimmy Learmouth was their chief comedian, and, obviously, although he may have occasionally used material from his own sketches, he was doing a great deal of spontaneous ad-libbing, and he was marvellous.

'He was a curious man, with a face rather like Winston Churchill, to which he often attached a very long, flowing moustache, that obviously did not belong to that face, and didn't even pretend to belong. I cannot describe his method, except that he was essentially a very funny man.

'I never met him, never saw him off-stage, but years later I had much to do with Julian Wylie, who was producing a dramatisation of *The Good Companions.* Wylie employed a large number of comedians and knew a lot about them. He always said that Jimmy Learmouth was the funniest and the best.

'I gather Learmouth was a very curious man, and, according to Wylie, drank an awful lot, as many of them did in those days. And Wylie said Jimmy had a curious habit of forever washing his hands – perhaps he felt guilty about being a comedian!

'Well, if he did, he had no need to at all. None at all.'

Norman **LONG** 1895-1952

A familiar figure walking the streets of Bradford in the early hours of the morning, accompanied by a Sealyham dog, was portly Norman Long.

This was in the 1930's when Mr Long was topping the bill at the city's Alhambra Theatre, on his tour of the Moss Empire's.

The entertainer at the piano suffered badly from insomnia, and his nocturnal strolls were well-known to the 'beat Bobby' in the vicinity of the Alexandra Hotel, where the top-line pro's invariably stayed.

But if Norman lost out on sleep, he certainly made up for it in popularity, for he lived up to his bill matter of 'A Song, a Smile and a Piano'. His act was full of wit and patter, as well as humourous songs he wrote himself, such as *I'll Never Love a Barmaid any More.*

The heavily-built entertainer at the piano was conscious of his toothy smile and portly presence, for he invariably commented as he made his stage entrance: 'You all know me – Norman Long – 'all Teeth and Trousers!'

This got him off to a good start with his audience. He followed this with a stiff bow, and elaborate ritual in adjusting the piano stool to just the right height, and making sure that the tails of his immaculate dress suit hung at the back at just the right angle.

However, what followed endeared him to his audience, for he had a pleasing voice, as well as complete mastery of the keyboard.

Born at Deal in Kent, the young Norman Long showed early aptitude as a pianist, and at the age of ten began the serious study of the violin as well, but he soon dropped this in favour of his beloved piano.

Upon leaving school his family insisted that he took 'a safe job' in an insurance broker's office. He hated this, but soon found an outlet by playing piano in a local dance band at weekends.

In the Summer of 1914 he took a job playing the piano for The Chocs concert party and this whetted his interest in show business, especially as he was being paid for doing a job he liked.

Then, when he got the offer of playing professionally for a touring company of Charles Heslop's Brownies he had no hesitation in throwing up his 'safe job' and joining the pierrots – the pay was better!

Norman Long continued to 'tickle the ivories' until he joined the Forces in 1916. He enlisted in the Infantry, but later transferred to the Royal Flying Corps, soon finding his feet (or perhaps his fingers?) playing in the squadron's concert party.

The Great War over, he added songs and patter to his piano act when he joined the Zeniths for a summer season at Clacton in 1919. His new act was so successful that from there he went 'on the Halls' making his first real stage appearance at the Lewisham Hippodrome.

Norman was one of the first entertainers to broadcast on the old 2LO Service put out from Marconi House in the Strand, London, in 1922. He proved popular and his 'Song, a Smile and a Piano' went out over the air for years.

However, his peak achievement in this field was the honour to be included in the first Royal Variety Performance ever to be broadcast – from the Victoria Palace – in 1927. When talking picture 'shorts' were made a few years later, he made many such films in the *Pathetone Parade* series.

Known as 'The Eligible Bachelor of Radio' Norman Long never married. He always said his only passion was golf and, invariably on tour, his first question upon arrival at a theatre would be to ask the whereabouts of the nearest course!

One of his quips was that 'he liked to keep in the swing' and in private life Norman was a very enthusiastic member of the VGS (Vaudeville Golfing Society.)

Perhaps Mr Long should have married a barmaid – for he loved pubs – or rather, good-class hotels. As it was, he had a share in the hotel his sister kept at Salcombe in Devon. It seemed the air down there agreed with him – much better than stuffy theatres – and there he could relax and sleep better.

Needless to say, there was a golf course within easy reach!

Arthur LUCAN 1885-1954

'Good evening blackguards, bodyguards and fireguards.
It's me, Old Mother Riley. Just blown in for a breath of fresh air.
How is everybody?'

Arthur Lucan, otherwise Old Mother Riley, is on stage at the Doncaster Grand in 1948. Soon he will be joined in the act by his wife and stage partner, Kitty McShane. Their relationship, both on stage and off, was of the fire-cracker variety.

Kitty enters to a round of applause: 'How long will supper be, mother dear?' 'About six inches, daughter. It's a sausage!'

A wave of laughter greets this sally. The stage act of 'Old Mother Riley and her Daughter Kitty' is a popular one, drawing full houses everywhere. Only fellow pro's knew of their turbulent domestic life, which had earned them nick-names like 'Alchoholic Arthur' and 'Keep him in Kitty'.

Born Arthur Towle near Boston, Lincolnshire, Arthur took his stage surname from the Lucan Dairy in Dublin, where he met his wife and stage partner Kitty McShane when touring with a fit-up Variety show in 1913. Kitty was only fifteen when they married, but together they formed a very successful stage act.

Before that, young Arthur Towle got theatrical aspirations when as a boy he got a job sweeping the stage at the old Shodfriars Hall in Boston, then running as a music hall. Later, in 1900, he began work for Harry Fountain at The Corn Exchange, later re-titled Boston New Theatre.

His stage debut was on the sands at Skegness, as one of Clement's Pierrots in 1902. Then he joined the Musical Cliftons, who performed at Blackpool and Llandudno, but 1910 saw him at Carnoustie in Scotland, as one of Gilbert Payne's White Coons. After touring in *The Honeymoon* in 1912 he was off to Ireland in 1913.

Back in England in 1920 Arthur Lucan was just an Irish character comedian in touring revue. His specialities were two sketches with Kitty, entitled 'The Matchseller' and 'Come Over'. Then he was taken under the wing of Lew Lake, who ran Collins Music Hall in Islington. Lew put Arthur in a revue titled *Irish Follies* in 1925 and this toured for years.

The sketch 'Come Over' impressed Lake, and as a result this was developed as 'Bridget's Night Out' in which Lucan and McShane (as they were now billed) were given a good spot in the Royal Variety Performance at the London Palladium in 1934. Following this, the sketch was re-titled 'Old Mother Riley and her Daughter Kitty'.

Lucan played Old Mother Riley drawing upon his experience as a Dame in pantomime. His first appearance in skirts had been at the Dublin Empire as 'Old Mother O'Flynn' and this character study formed the basis of the new stage act.

Old Mother Riley in the act was a belligerent but kindly old washerwoman – whose life evolved round her gin, her corsets, and her lovely but wayward daughter Kitty – played until a dangerously advanced age by Miss McShane.

In 1937 Producer John Argyle got the idea of putting Old Mother Riley into films, following a very successful Pathetone 'short'. Eventually fifteen pictures were made in the *Old Mother Riley* series, and they all made money.

Due to the hectic personal life of Lucan and McShane, it came as no surprise when they split up in 1951. Arthur Lucan then carried on the stage act with a new partner, but tragedy struck on the night of 17th May, 1954.

While waiting to go on stage at the Hull Tivoli in *Old Mother Riley in Paris,* Lucan collapsed and died. Ellis Ashton playing Mayor, then had the thankless task of announcing that an understudy would play the part, Frank Seton.

In his will, Arthur Lucan left his stage boots to another understudy – Roy Rolland – to 'carry on in my footsteps'. After that, Miss McShane revived the act with Roy Rolland playing *Old Mother Kelly* but she herself died in 1964.

A touching reminder of how much Arthur Lucan meant to the kiddies is the story that his grave, in Eastern Cemetery at Hull, is invariably covered with flowers. These, it seems, are put there by children who never knew him in life, but have seen his many films screened on television.

More ironic is the memory of Lucan's frequent tussles with Tipstaffs and Taxmen, and the fact that he had to appear at a bankruptcy hearing shortly before his death.

The Hull Tivoli Theatre had to close shortly after these events. It was demolished and on the site arose Tivoli House – home of the local Inland Revenue!

What an epitaph – a warren of Taxmen on the spot where Arthur Lucan died...

Enough to make Old Mother Riley *come over* all unnecessary!

Ted LUNE 1922-1968

If you were in a pub or club in West Lancashire in the early 1950's you may have been entertained by a lanky, bug-eyed comedian from Bolton, with accent to match, who recited in lugubrious style 'a letter from his Mum' which went something like this: 'Dear Son, I am writing this slowly, as I know you cannot read very fast. The woman next door has had all her teeth taken out and a new fireplace put in...'

And so it went on. The six-foot, ex-tool fitter, was making a bid for fame, above the clink of beer glasses, but away from the clatter of machinery.

In 1954 impresario Jack Taylor got Ted Lune a week's booking in Variety at the Hulme Hippodrome, a suburban Manchester hall. There he was seen in action by another Taylor – Ronnie Taylor of the BBC – who liked his style, and got him a part in a radio show titled *What Makes a Star?*

This led to further broadcasting committments, including top billing in *Variety Fanfare* and then in a series of his own called *Get Lune!*

Then it was back to Variety, and off he went on tour in a revue staged by Jack Gillam under the title *Peaches and Screams.*

In this concoction the Bolton lad made his entrance wearing a flat cap and carrying a daffodil (an outsize prop). His tag-line at this time went down very well. It was: 'I've been sent for – so I had to come!'

At one break in his act he would point at the audience and announce: 'You're wrong, you know. I *did* know who my father was. 'He was a soldier – Aye, name of KOYLI'.

There was a disappointment in store for Ted Lune when he got to the Dewsbury Empire in April, 1955 where he was billed as 'Joint Top of the Bill' with Issy Bonn, the Jewish comedian. They found on arrival that the theatre had closed down suddenly the Saturday before. The reason? No money in the kitty to pay the artistes!

Ted had to agree with Issy when the latter told pressmen: 'That's show business!'

But back in Blackpool the sun shone again, for that great Grand-Daddy of popular music Lawrence Wright (alias Horatio Nicholls) became interested in Ted.

Lawrie liked the Boltonian's homely 'off-the-cuff' style, and signed him up as leading comedian in his forthcoming *On With The Show* at the North Pier.

This venture proved a great success and Ted's salary went up with a bang for the 1956 season. So much so, that the saucer-eyed six-footer moved to Starr Gate (the 'posh' part) and bought his ex-dancer wife Valerie a Jaguar car.

Lawrence Wright, proud of his 'discovery' and his progress, quipped to the Press: 'I wish I could afford one!'

Now billed as 'The Lad From Lancashire' Ted Lune was certainly going places, and impresario Jimmy Brennan was quick to sign him up for the 1957 season in Blackpool at the Queen's Theatre,

as joint top of the bill with singer Barbara Law. Then, when comedian Norman Evans could not go on in *Hey, There!* at the South Pier, Mr Brennan had no hesitation in putting Ted Lune in to do the show, where he acquitted himself very well.

In fact 1958 was quite a year for the Bolton boy, for Frankie Vaughan, who was making a film titled *The Lady is a Square* got the lanky Ted a part in it.

He also took part in Harry Joseph's *Greatest Show of All* at the famous Leeds City Varieties. There he shared top billing with the great Jimmy James and Company.

But the biggest break of all came for Ted when he was signed up to play the part of Corporal Bone in the TV show *The Army Game* which ran to several series. This kept him busy, but the strain was beginning to tell on his puny frame.

The next news concerning the bug-eyed Boltonian was when he began to develop all sorts of allergies, together with bouts of bronchitis in the winter months.

In 1962 he had to leave the cast of the pantomime *Humpty-Dumpty* at the Liverpool Empire, when his bronchitis got so bad he could not continue. Then pneumonia developed and, although he pulled through, he never worked again.

Even Blackpool breezes could not put the lanky Lancastrian back on his feet.

Max MILLER 1895-1963

'As I always say, lady, some girls are like flowers – they grow wild in the woods
'Ere, did I tell you the one about the chorus girl who married a rich, old invalid?
She took him for better or worse. It turned out worse – he got better...'

Max Miller, a flamboyant figure in floral pattern plus-four suit, with white hat and red kipper tie, had the audience in his hand at the Holborn Empire, a venue he played many times until it was damaged by Hitler's bombs. Another Hall where Max could do no wrong was the Kingston Empire, scene of his early adventures in Variety from 1925.

The Miller man was a master of quick-fire patter. In this line he had no equal. Other comics went to see him!

The son of a Bethnal Green 'busker', Harry Sargent from Old Ford found he could make the troops laugh whilst serving in India with the Royal Field Artillery in the First War. From then on, he resolved to do nothing but entertain for a living, and not go back to his old job as golf caddy at Brighton.

Regarding the quick-fire patter, let Max himself explain how he came to be so good at it: 'I have been talking nineteen to the dozen since I was a Cockney kid. I watched the auctions in the Caledonia Market and learned a lot of patter. There they sell Christmas jewellery which turns green in the Spring!

'My father had been a comedian before he worked on the Railway, and had trunks full of songs, sketches and jokes. I learned to read music from an old cornet instruction book and by the time my voice broke I had a repertoire of heart-breaking ballads.

'My father made up his mind that I should learn a trade, and when we all went to Brighton to live, he had me apprenticed to a blacksmith. That didn't last long. I liked the golf course better...

'In the Army I was a 'bad lad'. This landed me 'in the clink' several times before I joined the unit's concert party, which was called The Lightnings after our shoulder flashes. I used Dad's old material and the patter picked up in the Caledonia Market to make me a comedian.

'They liked me, and when I got back to England I thought things would be easy. Easy? Little did I know! I have been learning ever since...'

Back in Brighton in 1919 Harry Sargent persuaded Jack Sheppard, who ran a concert party on The Madeira Lawns, to give him a job for the season. There Harry met Kitty Marsh, a contralto, who was to become his stage partner for a time, then his wife and manager. The year 1920 saw them touring with The Rogues concert party, and then with Gane and Morley's *Pierrot, Pierrette and a Piano* company.

While touring with the latter, they were seen by Ernest Binns, the northern theatrical impresario. The next season he booked Harry in at the Lidget Green Pavilion with his *Merrie Arcadians* when comedian Fred Miller left suddenly.

It was a case of 'Exit Fred Miller – enter Max Miller' who did very well at the Bradford venue. With the *Merrie Arcadians* Max was on £5 a week and 'shares', but at the height of his career Max Miller earned £1,000 a week at the London Palladium. In later years, Mr Binns treasured a silver cigarette case given to him by Max as a memento of that early booking.

Following Lidget Green, Max was launched into Variety and Revue, gaining experience in the latter with shows put on by Fred Karno and Tom Arnold. But it was not until George Black drew Francis Laidler's attention to him that Max Miller began to make any real impact on the music hall scene.

Laidler saw Miller working at the Holborn Empire in 1928. Max was wearing an old green plus-four suit and this gave Mr Laidler an idea. He immediately cast Max as the character 'Tipperary Tim' in a revue of that name he was staging, but had Max dress in a gaudy suit made of chintz material – plus-fours of course.

There had been a comedian on the Halls known as 'Hilton – The Chap in Chintz', and so was born the idea of Max Miller – The Cheekie Chappie! He was a riot in the 'Monte Carlo' scene, and Max kept the flowery suit get-up for his stand-up comedy act.

Later came the Royal Variety Shows – and trouble with various gags. Some of them came out of the 'Blue Book' when they had only been passed from the 'White Book', but to the masses that flocked to see him, Max could do no wrong!

Max Miller was genuinely sorry when the Holborn Empire was 'blitzed' and when Gertie Gitana – who reputedly read *The Financial Times* in bed – bought the Kingston Empire and then immediately sold it to a cinema syndicate, he protested: 'What are you trying to do to me Gertie? Render me home-less!'

Albert MODLEY 1901-1979

'Lancashire's Favourite Yorkshireman' was usually the bill matter of that grand little North Country comic Albert Modley.

Actually, both Liverpool and Barnsley claim him, for, as the pro's say, he was 'born in a suitcase' which means that his parents were on tour at the time. But wherever it was, Our Albert spent his early days in Ilkley, which is in Yorkshire, where he attended the National School.

He gagged about this, saying: 'If I had stayed twenty years I might have won a scholarship!'

Father was Professor Modley, who at one time toured the Halls with a companion as 'Modley and Partner', doing a strong man-cum-gymnastic act.

When Our Albert came along, father decided to buy a house in Ilkley and settle down. He picked one in Brewery Road (a likely spot) and fitted up the nearby Victoria Hall as a gymnasium. There, during the wrestling craze which swept Britain in the 1900's, Professor Modley trained aspirants for the stage.

The Professor gained quite a reputation, for even the great Eugene Sandow – the greatest Strong Man of all time – attended a course in Ilkley 'to learn showmanship'. To gain publicity for the Ilkley gym, the Professor took on the wrestler Hackenschmidt in a friendly bout staged in Wray's Pleasure Grounds.

In his dressing room at the Halifax Civic Theatre, shortly before he died, Albert Modley talked to the author about his early days in Ilkley. As a boy Albert, with his brother Allen, used to attend the old Grove Cinema in Ilkley, in company with a group of likely lads. This place was run by a coalman and was known to all the natives as 'Croft's'.

The cinema commissionaire (if that is the polite term for 'chucker out') was wise to the tricks of the lads, who often created a disturbance if the film broke down. For this reason he always insisted that they occupy the front row, where he could 'keep an eye on them'. This gave the boys stiff necks, looking up at the screen, and the sight of a bunch of youths walking round Ilkley looking skywards brought forth the obvious rejoinder from rival factions: 'Been to Croft's?'

Later on his brother Allen played the drums in the cinema, to accompany the silent pictures of those days. Albert also learned to play the drums, but was content to watch the pictures.

Our Albert's first job was as a parcels porter at Bradford's Forster Square Station. He was soon in hot water for allowing a prize pigeon to escape from its basket.

'I was only feeding it' he explained.

Then he got to entertaining his fellow railwaymen in the porter's room and, with one of them, Eddie Totty, they set about 'doing a turn' in the local pubs and clubs 'to earn a little beer money'.

Francis Laidler, the great Yorkshire impressario, heard of Albert and his talent, and found a part for him in his 1930 pantomime production of *Babes in the Wood* at the old Prince's Theatre in Bradford. Our Albert got £9 a week for his efforts and thought this riches indeed.

In this pantomime the famous 'tram act' was born, and forty years later it was still getting laughs. The very sight of Our Albert on stage with his drums was enough to raise the shout: 'Give us your tram act!'

For this, the little comedian let down a front cloth to the drums, painted like a tram front, complete with light and number. The cymbals and other impedimentia constituted the controllers and brake, and, with many a crash, thump and 'ting-a-ling' the 'tram' was soon well away.

Albert interpolated the proceedings with pungent patter, such as: 'Where are we going? Where the lines go, of course! And just to be sure we get there, we're following a bus marked 'Duplicate'!'

This grand little comedian wrote all his own material, and seldom used a script, for, he explained: 'He was never sure what he would say next!'

Albert made his home in Morecambe. He had lived there since the days of Ernest Binns and the Arcadian Follies when he was chief comic on the Central Pier.

He liked Morecambe. He said: 'The air is good, the food is good, and so is the beer!'

Just before Morecambe went 'Metro' they made him a Freeman of the Borough. He was 'fair capped' at this. When asked precisely what it meant, he replied: 'It means I can graze cattle on the sea front and ride on the buses for nowt!'

Dave MORRIS 1895-1960

The scene: The Market Place. The Mayor is selling off the Dame's effects to pay arrears of rent. Cedric (and a crowd of villagers) witness the auction, which at the moment revolves round what the Mayor describes as 'The Most Wonderful Fly Catcher'. This looks for all the world like a small pair of steps with a rung missing and a marble slab on top.

Says the Mayor: 'Now, I'll explain how this works. The fly leaves his lodgings in Moss Side.

He's on the move. He's emigrating to Upper Brook Street – the jam jars are bigger there. He's on safari...'

Interrupts Cedric: 'So far as he goes'.

The Mayor stops dead in his tracks, looks at the audience, and exclaims: 'Did you hear that? *Did you hear that?* So far as he goes...'

Then, turning to Cedric, the Mayor adds: 'One more crack like that my lad and you'll be playing Cynthia to Hylda Baker!'

This was only one of the hilarious scenes in the 1954/55 comedy pantomime at the former Manchester Hippodrome, which was Emile Littler's *Goody Two Shoes*. This pantomime was booked into the Hippodrome for eight weeks, but ran for sixteen.

One of the reasons for its success was that Dave Morris was playing the Mayor, with Phil Strickland as Dame and Joe Gladwin as Cedric.

This pantomime (one of the last staged at the Hippodrome) is still talked about. So is Dave Morris. Like the Hippodrome, he is no longer with us.

A very popular comedian, who everyone thought was a Lancastrian, but in reality was a Yorkshireman, Dave delighted in his deception. He lived in Blackpool so long that people thought him a native of the place. He plugged Blackpool at every opportunity. He even had 'Progress' (Blackpool's motto) stuck in his hat-band.

With his straw hat, thick glasses and big cigar, he was as familiar a sight on the Promenade as the seagulls.

Dave Morris, who joked his way through forty-six years of ill health, died with his one great ambition in life unfulfilled – to appear in a Royal Variety Performance. It was a bitter pill for Dave to swallow when he was rather pointedly not invited to take part in the first Royal Variety Show ever to be held in the North. This was the 1955 Performance at the New Opera House, Blackpool, in the presence of HM the Queen and the Duke of Edinburgh.

Dave had no time for 'broken-hearted clowns' in show business. He was as funny off-stage as he was on, and so was his brother Gus, also a comedian. Gus made his home in Liverpool, and when he had 'a week out' thought nothing of going on the markets, to 'earn a bob or two'. In fact Gus had such a strong line in comedy patter that the other market men packed up and went home when they saw him arrive!

The Morris brothers were natives of Middlesbrough, where their father was head cutter in the tailoring department of Newhouses'

store. Dave was inspired to go on the stage after seeing Pat Rafferty, an Irish comedian, perform at the Oxford Music Hall in Feversham Street. Father did not think much of the idea.

Dave made his stage debut in 1908 at a talent competition held at the Empire. He was thirteen at the time, and a barefoot newsboy, a familiar enough sight in the Albert Road district where the Morris family lived.

A tour with Phil Rees's Stable Boys troupe followed, then Dave was launched into Variety as a single act following an audition for Richard Thornton at the South Shields Empire. Old Dick Thornton gave him a piece of advice. It was: 'Never crack a dirty joke'. And Dave never did.

The First War interfered with Dave Morris's stage career in many ways. When he resumed in the 1920's Fred Waller, who was connected with the Blackpool Palace, helped him in his career. Dave did a soldier act until the topicality wore off.

Then he created his own individual style of comedy, and became well-known for his catch-phrase of: 'Don't laugh – meet the wife!'

Another catch-phrase of Dave's 'As'e bin in?' came much later, when he did the series *Club Night* on sound radio for the BBC. This was when he played the part of 'The Whacker' in the series about a popular working mens' club.

The little comic smiled, although racked with pain, for he was badly gassed whilst serving with the Green Howards in 1916. Later his eyesight became affected and he could not read scripts, even with the aid of his pebble-lensed glasses.

A reporter once asked him how he managed to perform, in view of his disabilities.

Dave blew smoke rings thoughtfully, then replied: 'Well, for a start, this cigar is primed with pot. Then, after a shot of benzedrine and a glass of coke, I hobble on with the aid of my stick. I do it because The Show Must Go On. And I go on because I need the money!'

Vic OLIVER 1898-1964

'You know, the hotel where I am staying is quite posh?
Yes, air-conditioned too – the manager breathes through
the keyholes every now and then... Don't encourage me!'
'Even the receptionist at the hotel is different – she has a
glass eye. How do I know? It came out in the conversation.'

'But it's the food. Ooh, the food. What a reputation. Yes,
they assure me it's untouched by human hand. Now I
know why – the chef's a gorilla!'
'You wonder why I keep moving around during my act?
I'll tell you – I'm no fool!'

A twiddle on the fiddle, a spatter of gags about Ben Lyon and *Hell's Angels* and it could only be 'The Old Vic' in the spotlight – Vic Oliver.

A very polished performer, Vic Oliver was born in Vienna, where he learned the piano as well as the violin. He studied music at the Vienna Conservatoire and became assistant conductor at the Graz Opera House.

Emigrating to the United States in 1922 he toured as a concert violinist, but when the 'talkies' came he added comedy to his solo act and toured the vaudeville theatres. When things got really bad, he became a musical clown for a time and even played piano in New York beer gardens.

His big break came in 1936 when he was seen by the great Arthur Schwartz – who had written musical numbers for Fred and Adele Astaire. Mr Schwartz thought Vic's act would fit into a musical revue he had been commissioned to write for the great C B Cochran. This was *Follow the Sun* and the story goes that Schwartz wrote the opening number for that show in just two hours!

Accordingly, Cochran booked Vic Oliver for *Follow the Sun* which starred Claire Luce, fresh from the *Ziegfeld Follies*. This opened at the Adelphi Theatre in London's West End and in the cast was Sarah Churchill, daughter of Sir Winston, and Sarah became Mrs Vic Oliver within a year.

The versatile Mr Oliver went on to further success by appearing in another West End revue for Mr Cochran. This was *Black Velvet* which opened at the London Hippodrome and starred teenage Pat Kirkwood who charmed everybody with her hit number *My Heart Belongs to Daddy.*

Cochran (known as 'Cocky' in the business) was pleased with his 'discoveries' and Oliver made a name for himself. He never lost his Austrian accent, which added to his natural charm. Vic's throw-away gag line: 'What has Paganini got that I haven't – except hair!' provided a clue to his appearance.

Vic Oliver's act was in great demand for cabaret, but he is best remembered for his appearances in *Hi Gang!* a War-time radio show which ran for years and did much to make audiences laugh when times were grim.

Hi Gang! – which embodied Vic's signature tune *I'm Just Wild about Harry!* - took the air for the first time in May, 1940.

Co-starring in the show were two former movie players – the man and wife team of Ben Lyon and Bebe Daniels. The whole production was a very slick, fast moving and 'Americanised' type of entertainment, new to British audiences.

Ben Lyon's main claim to fame had been his starring role in *Hell's Angels,* a film made by Howard Hughes, all about battling aircraft. The picture was originally made as a silent film, but Hughes decided to re-make it as a 'talkie'.

When this was announced, Ben Lyon suggested an unknown Jean Harlow for the feminine lead – which led to film fame for both of them. (This was why Vic Oliver constantly referred to *Hell's Angels* in his gags about Ben.)

Texas-born Bebe Daniels had sprung to fame with the film *Rio Rita* and she married Ben Lyon in 1930. They were known as 'Hollywood's Happiest Married Couple'. Like Vic Oliver, they had been in Britain since 1936 when they toured in Variety.

The *Hi Gang!* combination of 'Bebe, Vic and Ben' was very successful, but it was essentially a War-time show, and ended with a fan-fare, signing off in triumph with *Happy Days are Here Again!*

Vic Oliver was certainly a man of extremes. He loved classical music and in 1945 became involved with the formation of the British Symphony Orchestra. Later on he appeared in pantomime at the London Casino, and two Royal Variety Shows.

He died suddenly while touring South Africa, and left a niche in show business which has never been filled. There have been fiddling comics before and since, but none quite like Victor Van Samek, which was his real name...

Gilbert **PAYNE** 1877-1951

A prolific revue, pantomime and summer show producer, script-writer, and first-class comedian, was the show-biz track record of Gilbert Payne – who certainly lived up to his tag line of 'No Pleasure without Payne'.

Born in Leeds, he began his working life as a printer's devil, but following a stage debut in a talent competition at the local Princess' Palace in 1893, he began to think of the stage as a career. His chance came four years later, when he turned from type setting to setting out to show what he could do with his own type of entertainment. This was when he joined Monty Robey's Minstrels as a cornet player when they came to the Leeds Coliseum in 1897.

Touring with the Minstrels gave him valuable experience and, when minstrelsy stepped down in favour of pierrots, he stepped up to take the opportunity to form his own troupe of entertainers – Payne's White Coons – who played a dozen or so seasons at Scottish venues in the 1900's. These included troupes at Carnoustie, Broughty Ferry, and St Andrews.

While promoting and running these troupes he made several 'discoveries'. There was George Hirste – who made a name for himself on the stage – and Arthur Towle. The latter was with the Carnoustie White Coons of 1912 and he went on to change his name to Arthur Lucan, better known as 'Old Mother Riley'.

Payne was active in the pantomime field also, being a prolific writer of material, and this came to the notice of the great Florrie Forde. She commissioned him to write a special version of *Cinderella* which was a great attraction for the 1914/15 season at Glasgow's Pavilion Theatre. In this, Florrie played Prince Charming of Arcadia, while Payne wrote himself a part in the show as Pickles the Page. Following this success, other pantomimes followed for Miss Forde. He wrote several sketches for the music hall stage, appearing in them himself, perhaps the best remembered being 'Bingle's Bungle' and 'Checked Again!'

Musical comedy also came within his orbit, and *The Honeymoon,* a musical farce, had many revivals. In the first production in 1912 Payne himself took the main comedy role, ably supported by Arthur Towle as his feed and Geoffrey Earle as juvenile lead. The hit song from this show was *A Little Bit of Sugar for the Bird.* Other songs from the prolific Payne pen included *All the Best* and *You Can't Get Away from the Fact,* the latter being included in most of his shows.

After the First War, revues engaged his attention. Two he concocted and toured with being *Ninety in the Shade* and *Wedding Belles.* It was after appearing in the latter show at the Leeds Hippodrome in 1922 that he decided to take over the lease on the old Queen's Theatre in Holbeck.

This he did and, with the assistance of G W 'Phil' Ridler as manager, opened in July of that year with a season of stock company, followed by revue, pantomime and opera. However, the venture was short-lived, for several cinemas were built in the area. The great days of Holbeck Queens' were definitely over.

The last pantomime staged on the boards was *Dick Whittington* for 1922/23, written, staged and produced by Gilbert Payne. He appeared in the pantomime as well, and his cast included Louie Beckman, Marie McSweeney and Maudie Mack. Not long afterwards, the Holbeck Queens' was sold to become just another cinema.

Gilbert Payne – as usual – was quite undaunted. He promptly formed a great new double act for himself and a partner to play the Halls as Payne and MacNaghten. The latter was a Sheffield youngster who when the act eventually broke up, went on to find fame as Terry 'Toby Jug' Cantor. The manager, Phil Ridler, joined a cinema circuit, and for many years managed the huge 3,000-seater New Victoria in Bradford (nowadays the Odeon Twins).

Payne – after further adventures – recalled the old saying: 'If you can't beat 'em – join 'em – and promptly became a cinema manager himself, controlling several halls in the Midlands. However, he did come out of retirement during the Second War to promote live shows for ENSA.

Many stories were told by Gilbert Payne throughout his long career, and this makes it difficult to single one out, but one he was fond of telling concerns the time he was putting on stock company productions at the Holbeck Queens'.

His company had given *The Lady of Lyons* and he politely asked a patron having a drink in the circle bar after the show what he thought of the play.

The latter replied with true Yorkshire bluntness: 'Ah reckon nowt to it. Ah never saw no lions!'

Jack PLEASANTS 1875-1924

'Mary Ann, she's after me,
full of love, she seems to be,
My mother says, it's plain to see,
She wants me for her 'Young Man ...''

So warbled a comedian from Bradford with a
simple, droll style.

His name was Jack Pleasants, said to be a shy
lad, both on and off stage. In fact another of his
songs was titled *I'm Shy, Mary Ellen, I'm Shy* which is
more readily identified with him than *Mary Ann*.
This song was reputedly written for him by
Charlie Ridgwell over a pint in the *Duchess of Kent*,
one of Bradford's old-time singing rooms, before
its reconstruction as an ordinary public house in
1902.

But perhaps Jack's most famous song was *I'm
Twenty-one Today* which will be sung at 'coming out
parties' for generations to come. His number *I'm
Shy, Mary Ellen* is perpetuated by present-day
comedian Reg Dixon who has the singing rights.

Jack Pleasants was 'discovered' in the neighbouring city of Leeds, by the astute J C Whiteman, agent and booker for the Varieties, during 1901.

In Leeds Mr Whiteman organised 'Talent at the Taps' which meant talent nights in the tap room of the Scarborough Hotel in Bishopgate Street. Any artiste showing promise at any of these shows was promptly given a booking at Mr Fred Wood's City Palace of Varieties in Leeds, for which J C Whiteman was agent.

Jack Pleasants did very well at Mr Wood's hall, and a MacNaghten Tour was promptly arranged, appropriately opening at the Bradford Palace.

A correspondent wrote for the *Bradford Telegraph* at the time:

'At a Thursday matineee at the Bradford Palace early in 1902 the manager begged me to see and 'write a few lines' about a local lad who was making an appearance as a 'trial turn' that afternoon.

'At the back of the stage I was introduced to a shy, awkward lad who seemed 'fair capped' at the idea of getting into print. His efforts in the vocal and patter line had at that time been restricted to the Old Crown and other singing rooms in Bradford and Leeds.

'His name was Jack Pleasants and he lived with his mother in Whites View'.

And so the shy Bradford lad was launched on a music hall career which lasted a little over twenty years. His first appearance 'down south' was at Chatham.

Jack's first appearance in pantomime was in his native city. This was at the Theatre Royal for John Hart in 1907/8 when he played Muddles in *Goody Two Shoes*.

In this pantomime he introduced another winning song – *Watching the Trains Go By*.

His simple droll style went over well in the North, and one observer commented: 'Jack has the ability to convulse an audience with a well-timed shy glance'.

Jack is said to have been tutored in the gestures and shy glances that made him famous by his widowed mother, to whom he was devoted.

If 'The Bashful Comedian's' pantomime career began in Bradford, sadly it also ended there. He was playing Simple Simon in Francis Laidler's *Red Riding Hood* at the Prince's Theatre when he collapsed at the Boxing Day performance in 1923.

He was found to be suffering from appendicitis and John E Coyle, another comedian, was rushed to the Bradford Prince's to continue with the part.

On a brighter note, Jack Pleasants was fond of telling a true story concerning an engagement he did not fulfil.

It seems that early in his career he was appearing at the Argyle Theatre in Birkenhead, when he was asked if he would kindly 'do a turn' at a local Mission Concert, in between 'houses' at the theatre.

This he was pleased to do, and duly attended with his sheet of manuscript music.

A little girl was singing when Jack arrived, but Jack could not follow on, as the pianist was unable to decipher his hand-written sheet music. The curate's wife could not read it either, so a messenger was urgently dispatched to bring in the pianist from the Argyle public house nearby. In the meantime, the little girl filled in with a step-dance.

The pub pianist on arrival could not read music at all, but he could 'busk'.

He said: 'You begin, Mr Pleasants, and I will follow you with *Mary Ellen.*'

Jack had just made his long awaited entry when the call boy from the Argyle Theatre burst in and breathlessly announced: 'You are to return at once, Mr Pleasants. The Manager says you are due on stage in two minutes!'

Frank **RANDLE** 1901-1957

'Baa...Ah've supped some ale toneet...Aye, thirsty work this hikin'. Eeh, Ah've walked through Europe, Ireope, Syrup, Wallop an' Jollop, an me corns is givin' me gyp!

'Aye, Ah'm the Daddy of all hikers. Me, Ah'm eighty-two an' as fit as a fiddle, an' as lively as a cricket! Why, Ah'll tak' anybody on of me age an' weight, dead or alive, an' Ah'll run 'em, walk 'em, jump 'em fight 'em...Aye...An' Ah'll play 'em dominoes!

'An just look at these for a pair o' legs. Why, Ah tossed a sparrer for these, an' lost!'

Frank Randle is doing his Old Hiker speciality on the stage of the Accrington Hippodrome – his favourite theatre – one he thought of running himself, but never got round to doing so, due to failing health, in later years.

The time is 1951 and Randle is touring his own productions. This particular one is titled *Randle's Scandals* and he is surrounded by an army of stooges. These include Gus Aubrey, a drag artist, who was with him for years, Ernie Dale, Arthur Cannon and Stan Stafford, the latter billed as 'The Silver-voiced Navvy'.

Besides the well-known study of 'The Old Hiker', Randle did 'The Vulgar Boatman' and 'Grandpa's Birthday' all based upon real life characters. The Old Hiker was inspired by a veteran athlete who used to take part in the Manchester to Blackpool Whit Walk in the 1920's; the Boatman by an old salt Frank saw at Blackpool, and Grandpa by Randle's own grandfather, who lived in Higher Ince, near Wigan, where the Lancashire comedian was born.

Randle seemed inspired by spiky geriatrics. He had in his revue Pat Williams, reputed to be in his eighties, who was the surviving half of an act billed as Warden and Williams. He simply walked across the stage with a cup of water 'in case of fire'.

Known in 'the business' as 'The Stormy Petrel of Variety', Randle was very temperamental and a difficult man to work with. But he was a brilliant character comedian – a fact once noted by Gracie Fields – and commented upon by noted critic Hannen Swaffer who saw the comedian perform at the Kingston Empire.

If Randle had been born a bit earlier he would have made a fortune in silent films as a Keystone Cop, but as it was, his peculiar and rather vulgar type of humour was little appreciated beyond the North. A brave attempt by Jack Hylton to launch Randle in the West End in 1952 (in *Tele-Variety* at the Adelphi Theatre) folded after just two weeks, in spite of many changes.

Randle did make films, however. Trading as Mancunian Films with John Blakeley, many pictures were made on a shoe-string budget in a converted chapel studio in Dickenson Road, Manchester. These included the *Somewhere* series of the 1940's, with supporting artists like Harry Korris and Dan Young, and in one case, Diana Dors. Titles included *Somewhere on Leave, Somewhere in Camp* and *Somewhere in Politics.* Miss Dors was the counter attraction in *It's A Grand Life.* All these films made money when shown on the northern cinema circuits.

Frank Randle's real name was Arthur MacEvoy and as a youth of fifteen in Blackpool he was to be found in Gregory's Gymnasium at the back of the Tower, bouncing about on the trampoline, when not working as a waiter or bottle washer.

By 1918 he was sufficiently adept at acrobatics to join the Three Ernestos at the Tower Circus. (One of these was reputedly Billy Nelson, later with Duggie Wakefield and his Gang). His stage chance came in 1922 when he joined an acrobatic act in a revue called *Wild Oats* at the Accrington

Hippodrome. In this he was the 'Mac' portion of an act billed as Roy Brothers and Mac. This show was put on tour by Jack Taylor, later a big impresario in Blackpool.

In later revues called *Encore* and *Better Still* MacEvoy was known as 'Arthur Twist of The Bouncing Randles' but in 1928 Mark Ginsberg of Leeds gave him a chance as stand-up comic in his touring revue *And You.*

Ginsberg (later known as Monty Marks) did not think Arthur Twist a suitable name for a front-cloth comedian. He is said to have remarked: 'Let's be frank, it was all right for the Bouncing Randles. I know – that's it – Frank Randle!'

In this concoction, Frank Randle polished up his Old Hiker study, and in later revues came his other characters, which made him famous in the 1930's, onwards.

But Rubberface Randle's stage career was turbulent, to say the least. In 1954 he walked out of a pantomime at Oldham after only two days. The theatre closed! In private life he lived quitely with his wife Queenie in Blackpool's select Lytham Road.

Frank Randle's favourite gag (in the guise of the Old Hiker) was to appear undecided whether to blow a bugle or take a swig at a bottle of beer. Of course, the beer won, and this was the signal for one of his stooges to comment: 'That beer's thin'.

Randle's rejoinder was: 'Thar would be thin if thar had come up them theer pipes!'

Ted **RAY** 1906-1977

'King of the Quick Quips', 'Adept at the Ad-libs' and 'A Comedian's Comic' were some of the adjectives used to describe Ted Ray, who 'Fiddled and Fooled' on the British Variety stage for over forty years.

Born Charlie Olden in Wigan – the place itself the butt of a thousand music hall jokes – Ted got his own back by saying: 'I go down well in London, New York and Scunthorpe!'

The son of a ship's steward, as a youth Charlie Olden migrated to Liverpool and followed his father on the ocean liners playing the violin in ship's orchestras.

On dry land, he made his home in Liverpool when Jazon and Montgomery – who traded as The Liverpool Variety Agency – put him on their books at their Lime Street offices.

This followed the Wigan lad's stage debut at the old Prescot Palace – where he won a talent contest under the name of Hugh Nique – but wily old Jazon the agent insisted that he change his name, stop gagging and just play the violin.

The result was an engagement at the Lyric Theatre in Everton Valley, under the name of Nedlo, the Gypsy Violinist, dressed accordingly. (Nedlo was Olden spelled backwards.) The year was 1927 and Nedlo shared a dressing-room with a young Ben Warriss, then doing a black-faced solo act, not yet having teamed up with his cousin Jimmy Jewel as 'Jewel and Warriss'.

Agent Jazon got Nedlo other engagements locally at £7 the week, fiddling at places like the Clubmoor Cinema and the Olympia in the West Derby Road. At this period Nedlo lived in Anfield Road, within sight of the Liverpool Football Club ground. A youthful ambition of the Wigan musician had been to play football and perhaps get a trial with the famous club, but this did not happen.

Instead he turned to golf, and indeed became so enthusiastic that he took his final stage name from Ted Ray, winner of the 1920 American Open Golf Championship.

This came about when he was booked by a London agent after appearing as a 'trial turn' at the old Shoreditch Empire in 1930. The Empire was a London 'showcase' – perhaps the 'Opportunity Knocks' of its day – where all the agents viewed the 'hopefuls'.

His new agent George Barclay had different ideas about the act. It was: 'Get rid of the name Nedlo, keep the fiddling, but tell some gags – keep 'em happy!'

And so emerged Ted Ray, with 'Fiddling and Fooling' as his bill matter. His stage dress was now a lounge suit, topped by a trilby at a rakish angle, and 1932 saw an engagement at the famous London Palladium – way down the bill – but Ted was on his way.

In the late 1930's Ted Ray was in the £20 a week class – not bad in those days – and in 1940 he had become an attraction at the Duchess Theatre in the West End, appearing in *Beyond Compere,* his salary escalating accordingly.

Films next engaged Mr Ray's attention, but without doubt his greatest claim to fame was on sound radio, where his series *Ray's a Laugh* ran a longer period than Tommy Handley's *ITMA.* Ted's show began in 1949 and lasted ten years.

Many of its comical voices and characters went onto further success in show business. Ted's stage wife Kitty Bluett made good in Australia, Kenneth Connor found fame as one of the *Carry On* team, while singing duo Bob and Alf Pearson also did comedy, making 'Young Doctor

Hardcastle' a talking-point for years. Then there was Patricia Hayes, later well known for comedy roles on radio and television, and outstandingly as *Edna, the Inebriate Woman.*

The radio show *Ray's a Laugh* certainly made the Lancashire comedian's reputation as a clean, quick-fire gag type of comic. Ted continued to delight radio audiences with his part in *Jokers Wild* and *Does The Team Think.*

One critic said: 'His timing is flawless and the ad-lib comes second nature to him now'. Another scribe commented: 'This man was born with a gag in his mouth'

A reporter once asked him if he considered 1949 his greatest year (when he appeared in a Royal Variety Performance, and was also elected captain of the Vaudeville Golfing Society).

Ted replied: 'No. My greatest year was 1933 when I married Sybil'.

The comedian was also very proud of his two sons, Andrew *The Mudlark* Ray, and Robin, of *Face the Music* fame.

Someone once asked him the secret of his success, and Ted put this down to advice given to him by his parents back home in Wigan. Ted recalled how his mother had scrimped and saved to send him for violin lessons. She said 'Now you will always have a trade at your finger tips'.

His father's comment was: 'Save £1 if you earn £2, never eat fish on Mondays, and (most important of all) never play snooker with a left-handed Welsh miner!'

Armed with sound advice like this, how could Ted fail to raise a laugh?

J W **ROWLEY** 1847-1925

'Choose a starry night for a ramble... Through a shady dell
A starry night for a ramble... A kiss, and never tell!'

So sang J W Rowley, a popular favourite on the Halls for many years, and often billed as 'A Contemporary of The Great Leybourne'. His entry on stage at every performance was invariably greeted with cries of 'Starry Night'.

A speciality of this performer was his 'Going to the Derby' in which he appeared dressed as a jockey. His vocal rendition and ensuing patter was invariably followed by his 'Somersault Dance' which became quite famous.

In fact so well-known did the latter become, that audiences would invariably call out 'Over, Rowley' and 'over' he would go!

At one period of his career, he teamed up with the 'Double-Voiced Vocaliste' Ella Dean, and they appeared on many music hall bills together.

At the very first Royal Command Performance, held at the Palace Theatre, London, in 1912, Lancashire was very well represented by Harry Tate and Wilkie Bard, who both had solo 'spots' in the programme. But – as far as is known – the only prominent Yorkshireman to appear before Their Majesties King George V and Queen Mary was J W Rowley.

Then a spry sixty-five, Our John Willie had to be content with a place among the 'wines and spirits'. That is, a 'walking on' part amongst that vast gathering at the end of the programme, in a scene billed as 'Variety's Garden Party'. Nevertheless, he was very proud of the fact that he had appeared before their majesties, and never ceased to tell people of that great experience.

A native of Bradford originally, John Willie Rowley was at first apprenticed to a whitesmith, but in 1860 migrated with his family to Huddersfield. There he joined the Oddfellows, and became interested in the concerts they promoted at the old Albion Hotel in that town.

There he aspired to become a 'comique' in the style of the day, as fashioned by G H McDermott and George Leybourne, modelling himself on the latter. Later, comedy was added to the routine, not forgetting *Starry Night* and the famous 'Somersault Dance'.

Our John Willie, after some amateur experience, made his first professional appearance at Ben Sherwood's Gaiety Music Hall in Wakefield during 1870. For the next sixteen years he never looked back, touring the Halls with great success.

Then, for a decade (1887-1897), the popular J W Rowley tried his luck as a music hall proprietor, the venue being a wooden place in Huddersfield, now the town of his adoption. This place, a former circus in Byrom Street, was promptly dubbed 'Rowley's Empire' and he was reported to have lost money on the venture.

However, during his tenure of 'The Old Wooden Hut' he booked for a week in 1892 Charles Chaplin – Comic Singer, for a modest thirty shillings. At the time, the appearance in Huddersfield of the father of a little boy destined to become the worlds' greatest comic character, caused no comment whatsoever!

In 1897 when the Robinson Brothers (of Northern Theatres' fame) took over the old wooden Empire, J W Rowley went back on the Halls, singing his famous song and doing his notable dance as well as ever.

Not long after this, whilst appearing in pantomime at the old Alexandra Theatre in Sheffield, he met up with Ella Dean 'The Double-Voiced Vocaliste' whom he discovered singing in a weird place in an arcade, known as 'Cockayne's'.

Ella became his stage partner, and, following a notable success when they appeared together for Oswald Stoll on the opening bill at the Leicester Palace in 1901, they became a double act to be reckoned with on the northern music halls.

Following the 1912 appearance in the first Royal Variety Performance, J W Rowley settled down to live in Huddersfield, at a place appropriately called 'The Nest' in Swallow Street, where he ended his days in comfort.

However, in 1923, he was persuaded to come out of retirement and undertake a tour with his dear friend and former stage partner Ella Dean, in a show called *Veterans of Variety*. Later that year, the pair made another 'farewell appearance' with a brief appearance in pantomime at the Huddersfield Theatre Royal.

Rowley's son, billed as Bert Bond, also toured the Halls as a comedian, both as a solo act and with a partner 'Will Auster' as The Two Jays. Like his father, Bert soon became a favourite with northern audiences, but very wisely did not include in his act either *Starry Night* or the 'Somersault Dance'. They were quite rightly the exclusive property of Our John Willie...

Billy **RUSSELL** 1893-1971

"Ere, I say. Isn't this fuel crisis terrible?
Do you know, our house is so cold that the wife and I have to work up a heated argument to get warm..."

A stand-up comic with a difference was Billy Russell, whose bill matter bore the description: 'On Behalf of the Working Classes'.

He certainly looked the part – corduroy suit, trousers tied at the knee with string, battered trilby hat and usually with a red spotted handkerchief round his neck – but in real life Billy was the son of a Hertfordshire theatre proprietor, real name Brown.

The stage character he portrayed – Old Bill – was based on a pipe-sucking veteran of the Flanders mud, created during the First War by the famous cartoonist Bruce Bairnsfather. The cartoon caption read: 'If you know a better 'ole, go to it!'

On stage, Billy gave out with a string of gags about domestic matters, in a wheezy, high-pitched voice, as well as patter about working men, navvies, trade unions, and the like.

He was also master of the newspaper tag-line. During the last War, when he was touring the Halls, he would invariably read out: 'Old lady of ninety gives birth to twins', followed by: 'Hitler blames Churchill'.

Billy Russell made his first stage appearance early – at the age of seven – in a melodrama at Gloucester Theatre Royal. As a youth he met up with Bransby Williams, the noted character actor, and learned a lot from him.

Following this, the aspiring young character actor tried his luck at the Eastwood Empire and was delighted with a salary of £2 10s.

Then, after playing Ugly Sister in pantomime in company with Gus Grenville, the pair teamed up as 'Russell and Grenville', the original Russell having dropped out. They did a comedy routine and appeared in circuses.

When the First War came along Billy Russell (as he had become) joined the Army and the pair thus separated. Upon demobilisation, Billy found himself just another stand-up comic on the music halls, so he wrote himself what he described as 'Trench Philosophy Material'.

In 1919 he found himself in Birmingham, playing the Aston Hippodrome.

The open-top tram taking him to the theatre was held up, and Billy, looking down, saw a gang of navvies re-laying the track.

One of them looked up, wiping his brow, whereupon Billy exclaimed: 'Old Bill in Civvies!' And so the idea for a new act was born.

With his skill at characterisation, Billy aged himself by another forty years, made up with a red, bulbous nose, and added a sprouty walrus moustache.

The act 'On Behalf of the Working Classes' took shape, and Bruce Bairnsfather's Old Bill character brought to the music hall stage, clay pipe and all.

Old Bill was first tried out on the so-called 'Bread and Butter Tour' run by Alderman Broadhead of Blackpool. This syndicate of Halls were in workaday Lancashire towns, all within a few miles of one another, hence the nickname. A performer could get one set of digs and play the lot!

The Old Bill character was a great success, and Billy quipped to his friends that as time went by he needed less and less make-up!

Russell took his Old Bill character to South Africa, Australia and New Zealand down the years, as well as playing most of the music halls in this country. He also appeared in three Royal Variety Shows.

Billy was 'a music hall man' and had nothing but contempt for 'the clubs'. When, in the evening of his life, offers were made to him, he refused to play in 'those places'. Instead he made appearances on TV as a character actor.

Ironically, his last television appearance was as an old man in *The Pigeon Fancier* which was filmed at Eastwood, near Nottingham, the very place where he had made his first appearance on the stage more than sixty years before.

Stainless **STEPHEN** 1892-1971

'We're a great race, the British. All comrades, semi-colon. All shoulders to the wheel, semi-quaver.
We'll carry on until the Axis turns semi-turtle. And Hitler asks us for a full-stop — exclamation mark!'

A great exponent of this 'punctuated type' of humour was Stainless Stephen, a Yorkshireman from Sheffield, who served with distinction in the First War and did a great deal to raise moral in the Second.

The comedian from Fulwood conceived the idea of what he called 'audible punctuation' when he attended a course as an army signaller in 1915, and later used this type of utterance as his trade mark on the music halls – Great success!

Born Arthur Clifford Baines, he was a teacher at Crookes Endowed School in his native Sheffield, before he joined the Lancashire and Yorkshire Regiment when the First War broke out. He rose to be sergeant major and was twice wounded in action.

Later his brother joined him in the Forces, and together they wrote gags and sketches, performing in them at unit concerts.

In 1919 A C Baines resumed school-teaching, but a successful appearance in a concert promoted by the Sheffield Comrades' Association at the Temperance Hall, changed his life.

Topping the bill at that first 'Annual Armistice Night Concert' was music hall singer Clarice Mayne, accompanied by 'That' at the piano. 'That' turned out to be J W Tate (of the Wylie-Tate Organisation) and it was upon the advice of the latter that Baines became a semi-pro comedian, under the name of Arthur Clifford.

When the local BBC radio relay station (6FL in Spring Street) opened in January, 1923, Arthur Clifford was one of the first to broadcast. His gags and patter went down very well and he was soon in great demand locally as an 'after dinner' speaker. A year later he had progressed to be included as a 'guest artiste' broadcasting from the famous 2LO London radio station in The Strand, at Marconi House.

Arthur Clifford was thirty-four when he decided to become a full-time comedian on the music halls, under the extra-ordinary name of 'Stainless Stephen'.

This came about when he saw a suit of armour in a Sheffield shop and got the local firm of Firth, Vickers, Ltd to make him a stainless steel waistcoat. The firm were happy to do this, and let him use it as their trade mark, Arthur being presented with the waistcoat on the stage of the local Sheffield Empire.

Later, the effect was improved by the addition of a stainless steel hat-band; waistcoat buttons that lit up, and a revolving bow-tie – also luminous. With his 'punctuated patter' the music hall act of Stainless Stephen was truly electric!

By 1931 he was topping the bill at Barnsley Theatre Royal, where he was described as 'The Renowned Wireless Entertainer'. A year later he was voted 'Top Radio Comedian of 1932' in a poll conducted by a popular daily newspaper.

During the Second War he was active in Burma, entertaining the troops, as well as appearing at many bases in this country. Stainless Stephen was a great morale booster. He remained a staunch and life-long member of the British Legion, but never achieved his 'ambition' of giving a harpsichord recital at the Albert Hall!

In 1966 he had the startling experience of reading his own obituary notice!

This came about when the 'Live Letters' page of a popular newspaper reported a comment that he had died about 1960.

Stainless was quick to punctuate a reply:
'Dear Old Codgers,
You must excuse the writing, but according to your 'Live Letters' I have been dead six years, so you can't expect much!

I retired from the stage in 1952 and since 1954 have been living in Kent – a Gentleman Farmer – 'raising nothing but my hat!'
Stainless Stephen (semi-solvent)

The paper apologised, noting his famous sense of humour was 'as bright as ever!'

Before he did pass away (in 1971) he said in an interview: 'Yes. I'm Stainless Stephen. Stainless, painless, brainless, shameless, aimless, semi-conscious and approaching semi-dotage!'

A great comedian with a style all his own.

Harry **TATE** 1872-1940

'You're on, Mr Tate'. The call boy at the Mexborough Hippodrome is speaking. The year – around 1920.

Harry Tate, propping up the bar at the Montagu Arms, opposite the stage door, takes note. Downing his pint in one go, he attaches his outrageous and impossibly wiggly moustache, strides majestically through the door – and is *on* –

on stage, that is, talking glibly to his stooges about the joys of 'Motoring'.

How many performers could do that today? Precious few. But Harry Tate was exceptional. Did he not make King George V laugh in that first Royal Variety Command Performance at the Palace Theatre, London, with the very same sketch in 1912.

Born Ronald MacDonald Hutchinson, he began his working life as a post clerk in Manchester. But he soon showed exceptional talent as a mimic and got engagements in music halls.

Marie Lloyd gave him his stage name when he appeared on the same bill with her (as a supporting act) at the Camberwell Empire, early in 1898. This was his first London engagement.

Marie did not think much to the name 'Ronnie Hutchinson' so she asked about his early career. When she learned that he had worked for Messrs Tate and Lyle, the sugar refiners, she immediately came up with 'Harry Tate' after Henry Tate, founder of the firm.

What *the* Mr Tate thought about this arrangement is not known. Possibly the firm thought it a good advertisement, especially as Harry used it for forty years!

In his new career as an impressionist, Harry Tate evolved a scene called 'Number Seven' in which he did impressions of the leading comedians of the day, including George Robey, Joe Elvin and Eugene Stratton.

One of Harry's first engagements under his new name was at Leeds, where he appeared on the opening bill at the Empire, also in 1898. (He is said to have made quite an 'impression' with his impressions!)

In later years Mr Tate recalled this instance quite vividly, adding that he *cycled* from Manchester to Leeds to fulfil the engagement!

During the First War period, following his great success at the Palace Theatre in London, Harry Tate starred in several West End revues. The first was *Hullo, Tango!* at the Hippodrome in 1913, followed by *Razzle Dazzle* at the Empire two years later. As a revue star he added a catch-phrase 'I don't think!' which was quite the vogue for a time – especially when added to the end of a sentence.

But it was Wal Pink's famous sketch 'Motoring' that put Harry Tate among the immortals. A classic of cumulative chaos, it evolved round a car (inevitably numbered T8) which would not go – in spite of many 'Good-by-ees' from the occupants.

Tate owed a lot of the success he had with this sketch to the 'son' who made a wonderful foil – in reality a smart lad with a piping voice, named Tommy Tweedley – whom he had engaged whilst playing the Liverpool Empire.

There were others, of course, who took the parts of occupants, bystanders, and even a policeman who threatened to book Harry for furious driving!

Wal Pink wrote Tate other sketches, such as 'Fishing', 'Golfing' and 'Wireless', but nothing touched the priceless gem of 'Motoring' which was a riot while it lasted.

In the 1920's 'Selling a Car' became Harry's stock-in-trade, in which he was joined by his real son, Harry Tate Jnr. In this, one of the gags was when a potential buyer asks Harry: 'Have I met you somewhere before?'

To this, the comedian dryly replied: 'Possibly. I've been to Margate twice!'

Harry Tate's last appearance on any stage was at the King's Theatre, Dundee, in 1939, just after the Second War had broken out. Tate told pressmen at his hotel that he was 'resting' after being hit by shrapnel in an air raid.

As the 'Phoney War' period was still on, and no bombs had fallen, he did not expect to be taken seriously. But what a fuss there was when the 'news' broke!

Just like Harry to have the last laugh on everybody...

'For God's sake, get me off!' gasped the fat little man, who had collapsed amid the ruins of his deck chair absurdity, one Saturday night at the Halifax Palace.

Florence, his wife and stage partner, frantically signalled to the stage hands in the wings, shouted to musical director Vic Lewis in the orchestra pit, and, face blinded with tears, endeavoured to help. Hastily the curtain was lowered upon the scene.

The audience, after ten minutes of the little comic's clowning, thought it all part of the act, and applauded generously. But for little Tubby Turner it was no laughing matter. He had had a stroke.

Tubby, it transpired, had fulfilled his last engagement. The pathetic props were taken away, and the breathless stutter which had made him famous was heard no more on the stages of the northern music halls. His well-known catchphrase: 'If it's Ho-kay with you, then it's Ho-kay with me' died with him.

Born Clarence Turner at Great Harwood, near Blackburn, he was taken to Preston as a youngster. When he left school he got a job as a telegraphist in the local railway goods yards, and worked there until he was sixteen.

Then on holiday in Blackpool he applied for an audition at a show on the South Pier. He was lucky. He got the comedian's job – salary £2 10s a week.

In 1906 he married Florence Revill (of the famous Stockport theatrical family) and she became his stage wife in many of the comic sketches he wrote himself.

Later that giant of touring revue – ex-plasterer turned entrepreneur Tom Convery of Newcastle-upon-Tyne – put him in his famous show *On the Panel* which toured the Halls for years.

But the climax of Tubby Turner's stage career came when he was invited to play at the London Palladium for George Black. This was when the Crazy Gang were going strong there, and Tubby acquitted himself well. He proved himself every bit as funny as Naughton and Gold or Nervo and Knox.

It was in this show his famous deck chair absurdity was evolved, later to become an important part of his music hall act.

Tubby, with his ridiculously short trousers showing stripey stockings above sand shoes, and wearing a too-tight blazer and much-to-small boater, would come on stage with a deck chair.

Creating an illusion of the seaside by gazing at the audience as though looking out to sea, he would endeavour to put up the deck chair, although never quite succeeding.

After several minutes of exasperation, which had the audience in stitches, his wife Florence would come on. After watching his antics, she would exclaim: 'Why, there's no bottom in this deck chair.'

At this, Tubby Turner would point to his generous backside and protest: 'What the 'ell's this then?'

Another feature of Florence and Tubby's stage act – they were partners for forty-six years – was foolery with a harp and small organ. Attempts to produce harmony from these instruments would result in discord, both musically and between the couple.

One facet of the double act was Florence's attempt to recite, or as Tubby put it: 'To recitootle'.

She would enter and begin: 'My soul is in the mountains, My body is here in the vale...'

At this, Tubby would promptly interrupt with: 'What a job you must have – keeping body and soul together!'

In real life Tubby's interests were music and writing plays. He had just finished writing *Summat for Nowt,* a play which was subsequently put on by the Oldham Repertory Theatre Company, but sadly he never lived to see it staged.

Certainly in real life he himself never got anything for nothing.

Tubby Turner the comedian never quite made the 'big time', but he was always a riot on the northern music halls and is remembered with affection.

Duggie WAKEFIELD 1900-1951

'One, two, three...Where's my leg? How should I know!'
'Then how do I get out of this? It's easy – get your leg over!'

So went the conversation in a comedy scene entitled 'Leg Over' which was performed by Duggie Wakefield and his Gang in the 1930's.

Taking part were Duggie and his great pal Billy Nelson, as the inquisitive pair who donned the handcuffs in a police station, 'assisted' by Chuck O'Neill as the Bobby.

The act of Duggie Wakefield and his Gang was created by Archie Pitt. It grew out of some foolery in the touring revue *Boys Will Be Boys* put on the road in 1925. Archie teamed Duggie with Billy Nelson and the pair were a riot.

Later the idea was extended, Chuck O'Neill being brought in – hot from the Frank Randle stable – to make a trio of comedians. In fact, so successful was the idea that Duggie Wakefield and his Gang had a good spot in the 1931 Royal Variety Performance, held that year in the London Palladium.

Taking part in that 1931 show was Gracie Fields, who became Duggie's sister-in-law when the comedian married Edie Fields, Gracie's sister.

Two years later Duggie and his Gang were featured in the Gracie Fields film *This Week of Grace* and, in that same year of 1933, Duggie and Billy sailed to America to take part in a series of comedy films for ace producer Hal Roach.

In this country, Variety bookings for the Gang were in the hands of Bert Aza, the agent (Archie Pitt's brother), and they appeared many times with success at the then new Garrick Theatre in Southport. This theatre was billed as 'Britain's Best Variety Date' and the Aza agency had the sole booking rights.

Following the American adventure, Duggie and Company were featured in another Gracie Fields film in this country – *Look Up and Laugh* – made mostly on location in Blackpool. This picture had Our Gracie in the role of a mill girl and Duggie playing the part of a dude.

The last film made by Duggie Wakefield was *Calling All Crooks*, released in 1940, and made at the Dickenson Road studios in Manchester, by the Blakeley family. Arthur Mertz wrote the script for this picture – and the theme was a familiar one –

with Duggie in the part of a simpleton who triumphed.

Much of Duggie's success in films was due to his comic appearance, which had the natural aids of a tip-tilted nose and a 'tram-line' hair parting, not to mention a gormless expression.

In fact film critic Denis Norden once described the comedian's appeal as being due to his 'unorthodox distribution of countenance'. Asked to amplify this description, Norden added 'buck teeth and a gormless expression' and said that Wakefield was a singer 'doomed to be a comedian'.

This was quite true, for, prior to the First War, Duggie had been a boy soprano under the name of Albine Wakefield in productions staged by Gerald Mount, backed by the Carrie Laurie Juveniles. Like Duggie, they came from Sheffield.

In those early days Our Albine was managed by his mother, who travelled with him. Young Wakefield's stage career had been stimulated by winning a talent competition at the age of ten, in Bridlington, when on holiday.

Joining the Duke of Wellington's Regiment at the age of seventeen, Private Wakefield proceeded to serve King and Country. In 1920 he put himself at the service of agent Tom Convery, of Newcastle-upon-Tyne.

The result was four years solid work, as Jack Wakefield the Dude, in the Convery revue concoction *On the Dole,* supporting that great Geordie comedian Albert Burdon. Then came the Archie Pitt revues which led to the Gang idea.

Sadly, Duggie Wakefield's constitution would not stand up to non-stop work in revue, films and pantomime. He was taken ill whilst appearing in Jack Hylton's 1950/51 pantomime *Cinderella* at the New Theatre in Oxford.

Not long afterwards, the buck-toothed comedian who had progressed from singing at the Peoples' Palace in Bridlington to clowning at the London Palladium, took his last curtain call.

The Variety stage was all the poorer for his passing...

Harold **WALDEN** 1887-1955

'What has wings yet cannot fly?
The Bradford Palace of course!'

The band at the said Bradford Palace almost fell
off their seats with laughter when they first heard
this gag, cracked on stage by the locally-born
comedian Harold Walden in the 1930's.

It was a 'pro's gag' of course, and would be lost
upon the audience generally, as it referred to the
back-stage arrangements peculiar to the Bradford
Palace. This music hall (of happy memory) was
built directly beneath the Princes' Theatre, which
staged Repertory, an arrangement thought to be
unique in the annals of theatrical architecture.

On the Variety stage, Harold Walden had two
separate and distinct 'spots' in the programme.

The first was his 'anaemic footballer' act which
always went down well.

In this scene the Yorkshire comic came on
sporting his famous 'kiss curl' above a pallid white
face. He wore the claret and amber shirt of
Bradford City and carried a football. His outsize
'long-shorts' were at half-mast, and his football
boots looked much to big for him.

Harold made a diffident entry, quickly encouraged by shouts of 'Sign him on' from the band. After some patter, delivered in a 'sackless' style, he made a leisurely exit singing a song he had written himself, which was called *And Only Me Knows Why.*

For his second appearance, comedian Walden in complete contrast did a suave, 'straw hat routine' with very slick patter, closing with sophisticated songs at the piano.

This latter act had been evolved with the aid of an agent in Australia, who had advised Harold: 'Let the audience see you are not as simple as you look!'

Bradford-born Harold Walden lived in the Athol Road district of the city, before he moved to neighbouring Leeds. In his youth he only 'lived for football' and achieved his dream when he signed amateur forms for Halifax Town in 1911.

After playing a season for them at centre-forward, he was transferred to Bradford City, where he eventually turned professional.

This transfer followed an event of which Harold was very proud. In 1912 he was included in the team picked to represent Great Britain in Association Football at the Olympic Games, held that year in Stockholm. He was in the side which beat Denmark by four goals to two in the final, and received a presentation medal.

After five seasons playing football at Valley Parade for Bradford City, the centre-forward enlisted in the Bradford Pals (6th West Yorkshire Regiment) during the First War and rose to be a second lieutenant.

Following the War, northern impresario Ernest Binns recognised his potential as a comedian, and took him off to Morecambe to 'sign him on' for seasons of a very different sort as comic in his Arcadian Follies!

In 1920 Walden made his debut as a film star!

He was engaged by G B 'Bertie' Samuelson to play the male lead in *The Winning Goal* which was a screen adaptation of a play by Harold Brighouse called *The Game,* and most of the action was filmed at Griffin Park, home of Brentford Football Club.

The comic with the 'kiss curl' and the 'devastating dribble' had as his leading lady Maudie Dunham and in the cast were Alfred Drayton and Tom Reynolds. The film was all about two rival teams, and of course Walden scored the winning goal!

Then came Harold's tours of the world as a leading comedian. In 1925 he was engaged in Edgar Warwick's Concert Party which went to the Far East. Gwen Adeler (daughter of Edwin Adeler) was soubrette in this company and said afterwards: 'Harold Walden was the 'life and soul of the party'. He had us in stitches!'

Back home, the Yorkshire comedian toured the Halls with his act. He claimed to be the only performer to have won a medal at the Olympic Games. This he usually displayed in a glass case outside the theatre in which he was appearing.

A reporter once asked him why he changed from being a footballer to a Variety artiste. He replied: 'With football it's 45 minutes each half, rain or snow, with a ten minute interval, and a 'raspberry' from the crowd if you don't score.

'On the Halls it's ten minutes each show, with 'twice nightly', and a two hour interval in between. And there's a 'benefit' at the end of the week, whether you 'score' or not!'

Syd WALKER 1887-1945

'What would you do, Chums?'

During the last War a deep voice, speaking with an
East End accent, asked this question every week
over the air waves and created a national catchphrase.

The voice belonged to Syd Walker, the comedian, playing the part of an old Cockney junkman, in the BBC radio series *Band Wagon*. Also taking part were Arthur Askey (whose catch-phrase 'I Thank You' has also survived) and his partner, Richard 'Stinker' Murdoch.

Askey and Murdoch were supposed to occupy a flat on the roof of Broadcasting House and took part in a feature called 'Chestnut Corner' where ancient and hoary gags were trotted out week by week for another airing.

Syd Walker, on the other hand, had a spot to himself in the popular feature *Mr Walker wants to Know* which involved a weekly 'problem'. He took the part of the Cockney junkman, with 'homespun philosophy'.

After a stirring musical entry he would announce: 'Yes, it's yer old china Syd Walker, still seein' it through, Chums!'

He would then relate a problem 'episode' and invite his listeners to write in to the BBC 'advising him' on what action to take. His final remark was the keystone of the programme: 'What would you do, Chums?'

The series *Band Wagon* first went out over the air waves in 1938 and its success inspired the launching of a more sophisticated rival programme *ITMA* with Tommy Handley and Company.

Both shows were 'evacuated' to Bristol upon the outbreak of War in 1939 and, in October of that year, Mr Walker surprised West Country folk by reading the lesson at St Cuthbert's Church in Brislington.

On that occasion a packed congregation heard him preface the reading with his familiar radio greetings: 'Good evening, Chums. How are yer?'

Another aspect of his popular radio feature was when the Ministry of Supply became interested – from the wartime economy angle – and suggested that he use his act to popularise the National Salvage Campaign.

Syd promptly obliged by singing a song *Any old Rags, Bottles or Bones?* and exhorted his listeners to join 'The Make-do and Mend Brigade' in the interests of war-time economy.

The so-called Cockney comedian was no 'overnight success' for he had been on the stage since 1911 and was not even a Londoner! Although Syd lived in Chiswick a long time, he boasted he was 'The only Cockney born in Salford!'

This came about because both his parents were touring theatricals. After the pair had appeared in stock company at the old Prince of Wales's Theatre (better known as 'The Blood Tub') in Liverpool Road, Salford, his mother decided to remain in the city with her parents for her confinement.

It seems she was a member of the Kirkman family, who lived in Manchester Street, Salford, and it was here baby Syd first saw the light of day.

Like so many Lancashire comics, Syd Walker was given his first stage chance by the great Fred Karno. The latter ran what amounted to a 'repertory company' of comedians, all performing in various sketches and revues.

Before the First War Syd Walker was touring in the Karno sketch 'The Furniture Remover' (which probably inspired the junkman idea later), but by 1918 he was principal comedian for Karno in the revue *Stolen Fruit* at the Leeds Hippodrome.

At one period Syd was partner in a comedy duo billed as 'Walker and Lake' but by 1926 he had gone solo again in the Harry Norris revue *Stop Press* which was launched with a flourish at the Liverpool Hippodrome in West Derby Road.

The 1930's saw the versatile comedian elevated to West End status, when he played Ginkle in *White Horse Inn* at the London Coliseum, later going on tour.

Films followed this success, parts being taken in *Over She Goes* made in 1937, *Oh Boy!* in 1938, and inevitably *What Would You Do, Chums?* his last in 1939.

Following his radio career, Syd Walker had gone back to his old love, the stage. He was doing well as Idle Jack in the pantomime *Dick Whittington* in the 1944/45 season at the Grand Theatre in Croydon when he was taken ill, sadly never to resume.

Fred WALMSLEY 1879-1943

Three remarkable comedians were with the
Adeler and Sutton Pierrots who performed on the
South Pier at Blackpool between 1903 and 1906.

They were Bobby Allandale, Charlie Harvey
and Fred Walmsley. All of them went on to run
pierrot troupes of their own with great success.

Bobby Allandale teamed up with Ludwig
Blattner, the musician, to put a troupe into the
huge Olympia at Roundhay, near Leeds, for a
season or two before the First War; Charlie
Harvey, after adventures at Rhyl, toured with his
Victorians, while Fred Walmsley stayed in
Blackpool and formed the Tonics concert party.
Under his leadership they did a long stint on the
South Pier between 1914 and 1923.

With them for the first few seasons were two
remarkable 'discoveries'. They were Sydney
Howard – known as 'The Slow-witted Droll from
Yeadon' and his friend from Bolton, the
immaculately attired Terry Wilson, the light
comedian. Later on Roy Barbour, another comic,
joined them.

But the success of the Tonics depended largely on the personality of Fred Walmsley, a very individual type of comedian, and when he received a marvellous offer from Lawrence Wright, his old pal Charlie Harvey took over the Tonics and took them to New Brighton for a few more seasons.

Fred Walmsley hailed from Cranage, in Cheshire. As a youth in the family grocery business there, he was expected to give his mind to commercial matters, but his heart was not in it. Instead he was forever cracking gags and imitating popular performers of the day. Father said: 'You'll get nowhere with that nonsense', but he was wrong.

When father died, Fred sold the shop and made for New Brighton. There, in the Pier Hotel in 1900, he scraped acquaintance with Edwin Adeler, of the famous pierrot partnership of Adeler and Sutton.

The A and S Pierrots had made the Pier Pavilion their headquarters, and young Walmsley persuaded Edwin Adeler to give him an audition, the result being that he was recruited to the company.

By the time Adeler and Sutton had put a show on the South Pier at Blackpool, Fred Walmsley was quite a competent comedian. With his simple catch-phrase: 'Eeh, mother. Lewk at t'Tower!' he had his audiences in stitches.

Bobby Allandale assumed control of the Blackpool A and S Pierrots in 1907 and moved them to a small pavilion which had been erected at the shore end of the Central Pier. When they broke up in 1914 they had become known as The Central Pier Pierrots. At this time, Fred Walmsley broke away and formed his Tonics to play on the original pitch on the South Pier.

After the First War there was great rivalry between the Tonics and the Wylie-Tate Super Pierrots who had taken over concert party activity on the Central Pier, Bobby Allandale having gone on the music halls, partnered by Mae Ashe.

With the Super Pierrots was a grand little comedian named Jimmy Pullen who did a tram conductor speciality, singing his famous song: 'T'trolley's off t'Wire!'

However, Fred Walmsley went from strength to strength as a comedian with his Tonics, singing *Seven Years with the Wrong Woman,* and when the Blackpool Carnivals were revived in the early 1920's he formed a liaison with Doodles the Clown (William McAllister) from the Tower Circus.

Fred's popularity with Blackppl audiences was not overlooked by Lawrence Wright the great songwriter and impresario, the result being a tempting offer to join the latter's *On With The Show* at the new North Pier Pavilion in 1924, which he did.

Walmsley was a riot as leading comedian at this venue. In fact he was engaged every season until 1934 and became known as the 'King of the Pierrots'. He appeared in two thousand performances of *On With The Show* without missing one of them!

Then he decided to retire and take things easy. Some folk said this was just an excuse to spend more time on the golf course, for, like many members of the theatrical profession, he was a keen golfer. In fact so keen that his wife often complained about the number of cups he won, and called him 'Fairways Freddie'.

Late in life he cracked a true story gag which is still talked about in Blackpool.

He told a friend: 'I've been robbed of my appendix by a hospital specialist, relieved of my wallet on the promenade by a light-fingered specialist, and now another specialist has broken into my home in Second Avenue'.

When asked if the latter thief had taken any money, Fred replied indignantly: 'What? A comedian with money? You must be joking!'

Arthur WHITE 1872-1957

A ripple of laughter runs through the audience at the Palace Theatre in Blackpool, as two little men stagger on to the stage carrying a hugh roll of green baize. They are Arthur White and Willie 'Tich' Taylor, who, assisted by Bert Draper, are taking part in a hilarious sketch entitled 'Grace and Beauty'.

This 'cod' acrobatic act is one of the high-lights of a revue called *Arthur White's Scandals,* which is quite obviously a 'take-off' of the more famous *George White's Scandals,* so popular in America during the 1930's.

A small boy in the audience at the time – who grew up to be Sonny Roy, the comedian, describes what took place.

'In the sketch Arthur was dressed in a tiger-skin, big boots, and a deerstalker hat. Tich wore hob-nailed boots, checked shirt, and corduroy trousers, like a navvy.

'They would march on stage with a roll of green baize, and unroll it on the stage, at the same time informing the manager (played by Bert Draper) that they were a pair of acrobats who had come to do an audition.

'There wasn't a lot of dialogue in this sketch, but the 'business' and the expressions, and the whole absurdity of the situation, had the audience rocking in their seats.

'It was a really wonderful piece of miming by Arthur White and his partner, but of course they never got round to doing any acrobatics'.

This sketch stood Arthur White in good stead for many years, as did one called 'Miss Blossom's Guest House' and 'The Telegram Boy'. The latter was one by which the little comedian will always be remembered – about a tip expectant telegraph boy – also employing a great deal of mime as well as a very high standard of character acting.

Arthur White hailed from Bacup, in the Rossendale Valley, where he began his working life on the railway, as a porter at Bacup station.

One day the manager of the local theatre – John Walters of the Royal Court – saw him fooling about in the Market Place, twisting his legs in a peculiar manner, for the amusement of his cronies. The manager was impressed, and persuaded Arthur to take part in a talent competition, which he did, all for a shilling!

This incident whetted young White's interest in the theatre, and opportunity came his way when one of the Six Brothers Luck was taken ill and Arthur deputised. After that experience he spent all his time away from the railway working backstage at the Royal Court, learning all he could about comedy.

His big chance came in 1916 when Mr Ernest Dotteridge the agent, who also ran several theatres in nearby Oldham, signed him up to play a comic character called 'Sammy' in a play he was producing called *The Pride of Bizantia*. Arthur was a big success in this part and, when a tour was arranged, young White had no hesitation in breaking away from his job on the railway.

Mr Dotteridge was delighted with Arthur White's prowess as 'Sammy' so a comic character named 'Sammy Shuttleworth' was evolved to play in subsequent touring revues. The first of these *My Son, Sammy* toured for five years solid. Then came *Sammy in Society* which had a cast of thirty. This was launched by Mr Dotteridge in 1922 and this was still touring when the latter died in 1926.

Then Arthur White began to produce his own revues, recruiting his old friend 'Tich' Taylor, a 'club turn' from Bacup to appear with him in revue. Their partnership lasted 25 years and progressed from concoctions like *Pontoon Ltd* and *Blackpool Whirl* to *Arthur White's Scandals*.

In 1951 Jack Taylor, the Blackpool impresario, signed up Arthur White to appear in his revue *1001 Follies* and 'Tich Taylor went back to Bacup. The best of the White sketches went into the *1001 Follies* and other offerings were revived in the *Moulin Rouge* revue which followed it. At Christmas, 1952, Arthur White bid 'goodbye' to the stage after a final appearance in his favourite role as 'Sammy Crusoe' in *Robinson Crusoe* staged at the New Theatre in Crewe.

In spite of his stage successes, Arthur White always remained fascinated by the railway. In fact there is a story about him which suggests that he carried a copy of Bradshaw's Guide about with him – for light reading!

Robb WILTON 1882-1957

'The day War broke out, my missus said to me:
'You'll have to do something!'
'I said 'Who?' She said 'You' I said 'Oh!'
'She said: 'But what good are you? You're too old for
the Army, you'd be seasick in the Navy, and I'm, sure
the Air Force won't want you.'
'I said: 'I'll have to think of something".
'She said: 'You'd better. It's urgent."
'So I said: 'I know. I'll join the LDV – or the
Home Guard, perhaps.'
'She said: 'You! In the Home Guard?
What would you be guarding?'
'I said: 'Why. The Dog and Pullet, of course.'
'She said: 'Trust you! Would you be on your own?'
'I said: 'No. Of course not. There'd be me, and
Charlie Evans, and Harry Bates...'
'She said: 'How long would you be there?'
'I said: 'For the duration, of course. Unless it
finishes before then...'

In cold print Robb's monologue (which, from memory, went something like that) does not look much, but spoken by Robb, rubbing an anguished hand over his face, it was a celebrated theme – guaranteed to raise him a laugh on the music halls – and to endear him to millions via sound radio.

Robb, the comic genius from Merseyside (and you've got to be a comic to live there), delighted in robbing tragedy of its dignity. His scripts were his own. No team of gag men ever wrote him a line. He did not need them. His sketches contained portrayals of firemen, home guards, policemen, and even magistrates. And how Wilton put them over!

On stage fifty-nine years, Robb – real surname Smith – hailed from Everton, and began his stage career in stock company at the old Theatre Royal in Garston.

He left Liverpool to tour, and in 1903 met pretty Florence Palmer when appearing in a melodrama at the Alexandra Theatre in Hull. Robb married her, and when Florence died suddenly in 1956 it seemed the bottom dropped out of his world. He could only say: 'Without her I would never have made the top'.

It was Florence who encouraged him to try his luck on the music hall stage when melodramas lost their appeal. She gave him ideas for his act and appeared in his sketches, as required.

One of Robb Wilton's first music hall appearances was on the opening bill at the Dewsbury Empire at Bank Holiday, 1909, where he was billed as 'The Confidential Comedian'. He got no star rating, in fact in the pro's jargon his name was way down amongst the 'wines and spirits'. Robb himself gagged about this later. He said: 'I shared a line with the bioscope!'

From Dewsbury he went to Leeds, where, according to a correspondent, he paid ten shillings a week for his pro's digs, which was a small room known as 'a combined chat' (bed-sitting room). This had to accommodate himself, wife and baby, for the week, and they used the top of their prop basket for a table!

At this time Robb was engaged at the now famous Leeds City Varieties, at a salary of £6 a week, but after this he had no other date in his book.

The correspondent recalled: 'Fortunately he was seen there by Mr Tom Sherwood who then controlled the Opera House and the Empire theatres in Wakefield. Mr Sherwood was able to persuade a syndicate (Harry and Sidney Burns, the agents, then operating from premises in Albion Place in Leeds) to put Robb Wilton on with Star billing at the twenty Halls they then controlled in the North East.

'The tour began at Stockton Hippodrome and before it finished, Robb was booked to appear in London'.

The Liverpool comic was at this time doing his famous 'Fireman' sketch – 'Keep the fire going until we get there' – and this stood him in good stead for many years. And so Robb got his first stage 'break'. He was always grateful for Mr Sherwood's recommendation.

In later years his 'Magistrate' and 'Home Guard' sketches did a lot to raise morale and take the sting out of tragedy during the 1939-45 War.

After nearly sixty years on stage, he had just made up his mind to retire, when he was rushed to hospital. It proved too late.

They do not make 'em like Robb Wilton any more…

Wee Georgie WOOD 1895-1979

'Ooh. Mother. You DO look different tonight!'

Wee Georgie Wood, four-feet nine-inch wonder of the music halls, is standing on a chair on stage at the Bradford Alhambra in 1939.

He is having a good look at the features of Iris Sadler who, for one night only, is taking the part of his 'stage mother'. (Dolly Harmer, his regular partner in this role, had been taken ill and could not appear).

The difference in the two ladies was remarkable. Iris Sadler, a great comedienne, being tall and slim, whereas Dolly Harmer, equally talented, was plump and matronly.

Wee Georgie, often described as 'The Peter Pan of the Music Halls', had a liking for matronly ladies. Once, when appearing in a pantomime with Florrie Forde (who was buxom, to say the least) he sat on her knee in one scene.

Roars of laughter was the result. One critic reviewing the show wrote: 'He looked like a pea on a drum!'

But if the diminutive comedian was short in size, he certainly earned big money. When he was in his teens he was earning £150 a week – of which his mother allowed him to keep ten bob – and he was not unduly sensitive about his lack of inches. When, at seventeen, he was told he would remain forever 'four-feet, nine' he resigned himself to the fact, and cashed in on it.

In later years Georgie was fond of telling the story of how he was elected and made a 'Buffalo' in Sunderland. Robb Wilton, another comedian on the same bill at the Sunderland Empire, remarked: 'He isn't big enough to be made a 'Billy Goat!"

The little man with the big personality was born George Wood Bamlett at Jarrow, the son of a pawnbroker, and made his first stage appearance at the tender age of five.

This took place in 1900 when his mother took him to a Methodist jamboree in the old Jubilee Grounds at Seaham Harbour. Here Wee Georgie sang a little song *Skylark* in a piping voice and got a round of applause. His Auntie Maggie threw a half-penny onto the bandstand platform. This was followed by a shower of coins from all sides. When collected and added up, the amount was £12. Wee Georgie commented later: 'That twelve pounds deprived me of a normal childhood. My mother realised she had a gold mine in me...'

As a little boy, George Wood became interested in pierrots. He entered talent competitions with Leonard Thiel's *Arcadians* at Seaburn, and Leo Bliss's *Busy Bees* at Hartlepool, before joining Cosgrove and Burn's *Merry Mascots* for a season at Barnard Castle. (In later years Jack Cosgrove became Georgie's manager.)

At the age of ten, in 1906, Wee Georgie was a boy comedian with Levy and Cardwell's touring pantomime *Beauty and the Beast.* This had a notable cast in that May Gibson, playing the Fairy Queen, later married George Black, the great impresario, and Stan Jefferson, playing the Golliwog, was to emerge as Stan Laurel, film comedian, and the slimmer half of that wonderful screen pair Laurel and Hardy.

Former comedian Hal Gamble recalls going to school with Wee Georgie when the pantomime played the old Albert Theatre in Brighouse. Says Hal: 'Georgie sat next to me in class and I walked with him every day back to his digs in Elland Road'.

At thirteen 'George Wood – Boy Impressionist' made his debut on the Halls as a solo act at the Burnley Empire. Here he did impersonations of George Lashwood and Vesta Tilley and 'gained the plaudits of the populace' according to one critic.

In 1909 he was appearing at the Bradford Palace, doing his impressions, when he was seen by top agent George Edleston. The latter booked him for the Stoll Tour, and by 1915 Wee Georgie had appeared in New York at a salary of £100 a week.

Around 1917 Wee Georgie formed his Black Hand Gang to play the Halls at £150 a week, but his real break-through came in 1922 when he teamed up with Dolly Harmer who became his 'stage mother'. Their association lasted until her death in 1956.

By then the little comedian had become George Wood OBE and an author. As well as books he also wrote a weekly column for *The Stage,* the profession's own newspaper.

In 1974 he opened the Museum of Music Hall at Sunderland. When he left his hotel in the morning by taxi and told the driver his destination, the latter looked at him and remarked: 'My word. You're taking a chance, aren't you?'

left
Harry Tate
in 'Motoring',
Vernon Watson as
Nosmo King, and
Norman Long
'a Song a Smile
and a Piano'.

right
King and Queen
of the Carnival
Doodles and
Fred Walmsley
Blackpool 1923.

POST CARD

ADDRESS ONLY

To Hal Gamble
with the best wishes
of

Stainless
Stephen

left
Stainless Stephen
by himself, and
Ernest Binn's
'Merry Arcadians'
Concert Party 1923
at the Lidget Green
Pavilion near Bradford.
Max Miller is standing
at the back (centre)
with his hands on the
shoulders of his wife
Kathleen Marsh.

right
Frank Randle and
his wife Queenie 1950.

left
Jimmy Slater's
Super Follies at
Cleethorpes 1935.
Freddie Frinton is
the man on the left,
while the glamourous
blonde on the right
is Jimmy Slater!

right
'Happidrome'
Blackpool 1945.
Harry Korris,
Robbie Vincent and
Cecil Frederick.

left
Inset is Sgt Barnaby
Parsons AOC, 1918
with his wife, seven
daughters and two
sons. Charlie Parsons
is in the centre.

right
George Formby Jnr
with Beryl and
'Micky Dripping' 1927.

With all Good Wishes
Mr & Mrs George Formby &
Micky 1927.

below
Cousin Freddie's
Concert Party,
St Annes-on-Sea 1912.
Sydney Howard is
kneeling on the right,
Freddie Carlton on
the left, with Terry
Wilson standing
behind him.

right
This fine photograph
has been provided by
Peter Finn whose
father, Joseph Finn,
was stage electrician
at Bradford Palace
Theatre between the
Wars. It is made up
from 200 photographs
of Stars who appeared
at the theatre during
this period.

The author would like to thank the many people who have made this book possible. Although the actual writing took only a few months, years of research and personal interviews have gone into the work. The illustrations presented a big problem but, through the interest of collectors and others, a complete picture structure was built up. Few of the illustrations have appeared in print before.

For the illustrations then, thanks are due to J D Barritt, Ronald Bottomley, Geoffrey Clifton, Arthur Crabtree, D Forton, Graham Hall, Basil Hartley, Reginald Helley, Harry and Michael Joseph, Dolly McMaster, James Robertson, Maurice Robson, Mary Perrins, Ken Smith and David Harper. The magnificent montage of heads was supplied by Peter Finn.

Information about certain performers, including first-hand descriptions of their acts, has been provided by Gwen Adeler, Lily Austin, W W Lupton Brooks, Harold Dunham, Hal Gamble, Stuart Good, Rowland Hill, Arthur Jacobson, Steve King, Sonny Roy, Malcolm Rowley and Billy Whittaker.

Families connected with performers who have helped immensely include the Barnes family (Arthur White), the Emmott family (Joe King), the Gillin family (W E Gillin, the ventriloquist) not forgetting Mrs Eliza Formby (on both George Formbys).

Contributors sadly no longer with us, include the late Fred Hinchliffe (45 years drummer at Dewsbury Empire), Mary Martin (for many years with Grapho's Pierrots), J W F Lyons (Doncaster journalist and theatrical reviewer), and George Wood OBE who performed as Wee Georgie Wood, wrote for *The Stage* newspaper, and corresponded with the author for years, as well as granting several personal interviews.

The various Music Hall Associations have been most helpful, in particular Joe Ging (of the Northern Music Hall Association at Newcastle), Harry Snape (North Staffordshire MHA), Trevor Lee and Eric Broomhead (Nottingham and Derby MHA), Ellis Ashton (British Music Hall Society), and Irving Mendelsohn, Gerry Collins, Geoff Lord, Fred Amos and Malcolm Airey (all of the Manchester MHA).

In addition, Cyril Critchlow who runs the Museum of Entertainment in Coronoation Street, Blackpool, has been of great assistance in regard to aspects of that popular resort and its performers down the years.

The cartoons used in the work were drawn by the author, with artistic advice from Tim Clapham. The exception was the picture of Stainless Stephen whose caricature was drawn by the performer himself, and presented to Hal Gamble.

Gentlemen of the Press whose co-operation is thankfully acknowledged include Peter Hepple, editor of *The Stage*, J O Blake, editor of *Call Boy*, and Tony Barker, editor of *Music Hall*. Also Robin Duke of the *Blackpool Gazette* who supplied the Dave Morris photograph, Nigel M Anderson *Chelsea News*, Harold Winpenny *Halifax Courier*, Derek Naylor *Yorkshire Evening Post* and Peter Holdsworth *Bradford Telegraph and Argus*.

The author would also like to thank reference librarians in various towns and cities in the North who have been very helpful in supplying information.

Grateful thanks are due to J B Priestley and BBC Newcastle for their permission to use material relative to Jimmy Learmouth in this work.

Acknowledgement is also made to Daniel Farson in regard to Billy Danvers.

Arthur Askey CBE provided the foreword, and his own catch-phrase 'I Thank You' is due to him appropriately in this respect, while more thanks are due to Dickie Henderson OBE for his kindness in writing an introductory tribute to his late father, Dick Henderson, who figures in the book.

Finally a very big 'Thank You' to George Kelsall who gave me the idea for *They Made Us Laugh* and also undertook the formidable task of publishing it.

Geoff Mellor